A CREATIVE GUIDE TO
ARRANGING FLOWERS

A CREATIVE GUIDE TO
ARRANGING FLOWERS

PAMELA WESTLAND & MADGE GREEN

with an introduction by
HANNAH GORDON

GALLERY BOOKS
An Imprint of W. H. Smith Publishers Inc.
112 Madison Avenue
New York City 10016

Illustrations by Charles Raymond and Claire Davies

Special photography by Paul Williams and Pete Jones

Published in the United States of America by Gallery Books
An imprint of W.H. Smith Publishers Inc.
112 Madison Avenue, New York, N.Y. 10016.

Copyright © 1984 Orbis Publishing Limited
Text © 1984 by Pamela Westland and Madge Green

First published in Great Britain by Orbis Publishing Limited,
London 1984.

Printed in Italy

ISBN: 0-8317-0414-4

1 2 3 4 5 6 7 8 9 10

CONTENTS

INTRODUCTION 7

FIRST THINGS FIRST 9

FLOWERS FOR THE HOME 27

FLOWERS FOR SPECIAL OCCASIONS 41

FLOWERS TO CARRY AND WEAR 63

FLOWERS FOR DISPLAY 77

EVERLASTING BEAUTY 85

CONTAINERS AND EQUIPMENT 99

A – Z IDEAL PLANTS 107

USEFUL ADDRESSES 123

GLOSSARY 124

INDEX 125

ACKNOWLEDGMENTS 128

Flowers are important to me. The scent, colour and shape of them can transform a room, make a guest feel really welcome, turn a simple straw hat into something special and add a touch of festivity to any occasion.

I'm lucky enough to have a garden — and a wonderful parsley grower in my son Ben — but I still find flower shops and stalls irresistible. Fortunately it only takes a few flowers in the house to make me feel good, so the way they are arranged really matters.

My preference is for flowers to look as natural as possible. But I've learnt that something which looks very simple and effortless — whether a flower arrangement or a stage performance — is usually the product of experience, training, hard work, natural flair, and a few trade secrets! What flowers you use, where you put them, and which container you choose, are just a few of the things which can make the difference between what looks like a random bunch plonked in the nearest available jar, and a simple but effective display that will give days of pleasure.

Like most people these days, my schedule is pretty hectic — juggling my family's needs with those of a demanding career as an actress — and I've never had time to go to classes to learn how to arrange flowers. So I particularly appreciated being able to read, at times which suited me, the very practical advice and inspirational ideas of our two authors, Pamela Westland and Madge Green.

Whether it is tips on which flowers to plant, buy and preserve, how and when to cut them or what to look for when buying flowers from florists that you need, the information is here. Hints on making cut flowers last longer — a subject dear to my heart — wiring them for greater flexibility, and using containers and equipment to the greatest advantage, are all given clearly and simply with helpful illustrations. The importance of colour, shape and style is discussed in a practical way, that is, so that you can suit your arrangements to the occasion and the setting.

The enthusiasm stimulated by this combination of advice and ideas is part of the satisfaction you gain from working with beautiful, natural materials. It is a satisfaction which increases the more you learn about growing and arranging flowers — a pastime which requires no special talent, does not have to be either time-consuming or expensive, and is related to many other interests. I also enjoy growing the plants, looking through old junk shops for 'finds' in which to put my arrangements, and the pleasure that these arrangements give to my family and friends.

I hope this book will help you share my pleasure in growing, arranging and appreciating the flowers and foliage which surround us.

Hannah Gordon

FIRST THINGS FIRST

The natural grace of flowers and foliage is always visible, even if you do no more than put them in a vase to arch, tumble or trail where they will. But haven't you wondered, on receiving an elegant bouquet, or when picking summer garden flowers, how you could create that striking effect you can see in your mind's eye, or make the freshness of newly-cut blooms last a little bit longer? The following pages give you the advice you need on conditioning plant materials and on basic techniques of arranging them, so they will give of their best for as long as possible.

Many details contribute to the proper care of cut flowers and foliage. They start with how and when to pick, recognizing the best buys at the florist, and what to do when you bring the flowers indoors. When you make an arrangement it is important to appreciate the natural growth pattern of each stem, to contrive an effect that looks true to nature.

Start with the basics – the flowers most readily available in each season and some simple ideas on presentation. Then discover how you can add or improvise to ensure an eye-catching display for any and every room in your home, all the year round.

There's a knock on the door, and suddenly you're the proud possessor of a beautiful surprise bouquet! After the initial excitement and delight, what can you do to make sure you enjoy the flowers at their best?

First remove the paper and ribbon bows, strip off any low leaves on the stems and stand the flowers in a bucket of tepid water to have a good, long drink; they are best left overnight.

The spray may have been made up to special instructions and designed in colours chosen to match a room in your home, but it is more likely that you will receive a mixed bunch of lovely seasonal flowers. Take careful note of the colour and type of flowers, and consider whether they might best be displayed in two separate arrangements. There may be irises, carnations and single chrysanthemums that would make a beautiful group for the living room, and scented freesias that you could extract as a personal luxury for your bedroom. Or you may find that nestling among a bunch of brilliantly coloured spring daffodils and tulips are a few hothouse carnations or gerberas which, with the addition of some graceful foliage, would make an elegant centrepiece for the dining table.

Usually the bouquet will include some sprays of leaves — privet and maidenhair fern are popular choices. Add other leaves of different shapes and textures if you can, sprays of spotted laurel or single hosta leaves from the garden, trails of ivy or weeping fig leaves from houseplants. Stand these in water, too.

The fact that a spray of flowers is long and narrow certainly does not mean that you must make the arrangement in a tall, upright vase. Indeed, one of the hardest and earliest lessons to learn is that stems are made to be shortened! Usually a flower spray made up by a florist will consist of very tall materials at the back — gladioli, irises or sprays of single chrysanthemums — with stems of graduating height, down to very short ones, in the front.

If you receive a lovely bouquet, like the one shown in detail opposite, you could put all the flowers in one basket, making a lavish but informal display for a hall table or windowsill. Alternatively you can divide the flowers into two colour groups, as below, pink, white and cream for a summery lunch table, and cool blue, mauve and cream to highlight a coffee table.

TWO
ARRANGEMENTS
FROM THE SINGLE
BOUQUET

THE BOUQUET DISPLAYED

For long-lasting fresh flower arrangements with all the materials looking their very best, you must take special care at three stages: when you cut or choose the flowers and foliage, when you condition them to their new way of life and, which is just as important, during the lifetime of the arrangement.

When to pick

Plant material is best picked in the coolness of early morning, when it is crisp and supercharged with moisture, or at the end of the day when its food reserves are highest. If you must pick during the day, try to do so after light rain, when skies are overcast, or gather only flowers which have been out of full sunlight for an hour or so. Avoid picking in very hot, frosty, or blustery weather or after prolonged rain.

How to pick

Always try to put cut items straight into a bucket of *warm* water, taken into the garden with you. If you cut straight into water you can usually arrange the flowers at once and get away with very little other pre-arrangement care.

Sever each flower or leaf from the plant with a sharp knife or scissors, making a clean slanting cut (fig.1). The purpose of this is to increase the cut surface area and thus the ability of the plant to take up water. Hard woody-stemmed items such as roses, chrysanthemums and flowers or leaves from shrubs seem to benefit from having the lower part of their cut stems well crushed. Beat an inch or so at the base of the stem with a hammer or a stone; slim stems can be hit with the handles of the scissors. This rough treatment appears to help the more difficult flowers and branches to take up water.

Remove thorns from roses by rubbing the back of your scissors very vigorously up and down the stems. Not only does this prevent you scratching your fingers but if chicken wire is being used to hold the stems in an arrangement there are no thorns to become snagged tiresomely in the wire. Plants lose moisture through their leaves, so remove any excess foliage from stems. Also, strip off any leaves which might go under the water in the arrangement; these otherwise contaminate the water as they decay. Take all the leaves from such notoriously difficult material as cut lilac, mock orange

(*Philadelphus*) and clematis. If you do all this while you are still in the garden, it saves making a mess indoors. Bring the flowers indoors and keep them in a cool, shady place for several hours before arranging.

Slight adaptation is needed for wayside walks. For the bucket of water, substitute large polythene bags filled with damp tissues. Put the cut flowers straight into the bags, seal the tops and keep them as cool as possible. Wrap branches of leaves in wet newspaper. Put the materials into water as soon as you get home.

Buying flowers

Always try to shop at a florist's where there is a reasonably quick turnover. Monday morning is a bad time to buy flowers as they are not usually fresh.

In the shop, take a good look into the buckets and vases. All petals and leaves should look pristine and fresh and the whole bunch should have a generally lively air. Stems should snap crisply and be clean and free of slime. Look into the centres of any open blooms; pollen colour changes from light yellow to a darker golden colour when the flower is getting old. The pollen should not be starting to shed.

Big double chrysanthemum blooms have a kind of dimple in the middle while they are still young: carnations should have petals still curled over in the centres. Avoid any flowers which are even slightly suspect. For instance, chrysanthemums which have had all the foliage removed from their stems are of doubtful value (though the florist will often have removed excess foliage from roses — that is acceptable).

Buds are a good buy if they are already showing the colour of the flower. Buds which are too tight and immaturely green may never open properly, though gladioli are an exception. If you need gladioli for a special occasion order them in good time and tell the florist what day you want them to be at perfection. They can be coaxed into full flower from green sticks within a few days if brought into a light, warm atmosphere.

Carnation and chrysanthemum sprays are good investments because you get lots of blooms and buds for your cash, though paying only for the one long single main stalk. Clever shoppers choose the stems carrying the most buds and flowers. These are attractive in a large display, or it is easy to cut the spray into a number of separate shorter stems.

Florists' flowers should last well, often better than the same kinds home-grown; healthy long-lasting varieties with built-in sturdiness are important to a good florist. Some exotics such as *Protea*, *Strelitzia*, amaryllis and many kinds of orchid make particularly splendid buys, principally because they are naturally long-lasting as cut flowers. The two first flowers mentioned will also dry off while in an arrangement and then last indefinitely. Such flowers may seem an expensive outlay but are in reality very economical. Florist's shop foliage, such as eucalyptus, grevillea, and the soft, blue-grey reindeer moss, lasts for ages and is well worth seeking out.

Although they do not have time for fussy mothering of cut flowers, good florists will have dealt with the blooms in their care knowledgeably and well, so that everything you buy should be at shining perfection when you get it home. When you reach home, flowers and leaves should not be left out of water any longer than is absolutely necessary. If you cannot start your arrangement at once, leave the bunch in water in a cool dark place. Re-cut the bottoms of all the stems with a slanting cut before arranging as this exposes more of the inner drinking cells to the water (fig 1).

Treatment of flowers and foliage

To condition plant material so that it has the longest possible life means taking measures to ensure that each flower-head or leaf is drawing up sufficient moisture to prevent it from wilting or dying prematurely. You are halfway to success if you follow the earlier suggestions (especially by picking straight into water), but some flowers and leaves need extra care.

Very often wilting or the early demise of a flower is caused by an air-lock that has formed in the stem, blocking the water intake. That is why it is always helpful to cut stems under water — even when you are shortening them to the required length for an arrangement.

In bad cases of wilting, wrap tissues under the flower heads to protect them from steam and dip the stem ends in a pan containing 2.5cm (1 in) of boiling water, for one minute. Or, as first-aid of a different kind, hold the flowers heads down over the sink and sprinkle them with cool water from a watering can. Alternatively float them in water. In each case, after the treatment, wrap the stems closely in newspaper, leaving the flower

fig 1   fig 2

heads exposed, and let them stand for an hour or so with the entire length of the stems in warm water.

Boiling water treatment is beneficial for all material with woody stems, such as roses, lilac, chrysanthemums and foliage sprays. Scrape away 5cm (2 in) of bark at the base of the stems. Split the stem ends, using secateurs or a very sharp knife (fig 2) or lightly tap them with a wooden mallet or hammer to crush them (but not to pulverize them!). Put the crushed ends in shallow boiling water and leave to cool, then place in a bucket filled with cold water for a long drink.

Foliage can benefit from being completely immersed in water — it absorbs moisture through the leaf tissues. Leave mature sprays in water overnight, but young foliage for no more than two hours.

Stems which 'bleed' and exude a milky fluid, such as euphorbias, poinsettias and poppies, are singed to prevent the fluid from hardening and blocking the water intake. Cut the stems at an angle and hold them over a match, candle or gas flame for 30 seconds to seal them (fig 3), then stand them in warm water. Repeat this simple but vital performance if you re-cut the stems. As an extra precaution you can prick the stems with a sterilized needle just below the flower head (fig 4), to release any trapped air.

Dahlias and some other summer flowers seem to last longer if the stems are first dipped into cooking salt, which acts as a disinfectant and assists water intake.

Tulips are always considered a special case, as they are surely the most wayward and disobedient of flowers. Wrap the stems in paper and stand them in warm water (fig 5) for several hours in order to straighten the stalks.

Inside tips

There are a few extra hints and tips, some with almost the status of old wives' tales, which are worth trying, to prolong the life of cut fresh flowers. To freshen wild flowers (often the fastest to fade), wipe the stems completely dry, then dip them in vinegar for a couple of minutes. Rose, honeysuckle, Solomon's seal and hosta stems can be dipped for no more than five seconds, in oil of peppermint (available in minute quantities from chemists).

When arranging roses, dissolve 5ml (1 tsp) sugar or glucose, or an aspirin tablet, in warm water and add it to the container. Or try one of the proprietary brands of cut flower food.

Metal containers, such as silver and copper, seem to help preserve cut flowers. It is thought that these substances inhibit bacteria growth.

Hygiene

Nothing beats pure water for keeping plant materials fresh and healthy. It goes without saying that all containers, pinholders, wire netting and other items should be thoroughly scrubbed, rinsed and dried before being stored. A little bleach in the washing water helps to remove any residual grime. To clean stains from glass containers, half-fill them with soapy water, add a few spoons of raw rice — never sand — and swish them about. The rice acts as a mild and effective abrasive.

To keep the water clear when you arrange members of the *brassica* family — ornamental cabbage for example — you can add a few drops of disinfectant or bleach to the water.

Transporting flowers

When picking a homely bunch of garden flowers to give to a friend it is a good idea to arrange the blooms posy-fashion in the hand — tallish stems in the middle

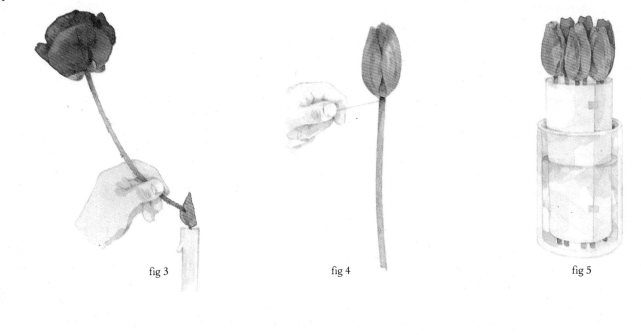

fig 3   fig 4   fig 5

or at the back, shorter ones round the sides, perhaps with a collar of leaves. Tie the stems firmly together with soft darning wool then put the whole bunch into a large plastic bag. The trick is to blow air into the bag before inserting the flowers and afterwards tie it like a balloon. The 'balloon' seals in moisture and also acts as a buffer against knocks. Alternatively, you can carry a posy flat in a box or basket.

Take a tip from florists when transporting flowers, leaves and other items which you want to arrange on arrival. Pack them firmly but gently into a cardboard flower box. These boxes are long and shallow, with lids. Beg one from a friendly florist. When packing, put in the long stems first. Individual leaves can be packed together in small plastic bags, kept flat. Flowers can also be transported in a bucket half-filled with water and held firmly inside a suitable box, packed round with newspaper so it cannot fall over.

Carry sturdy wild flowers wrapped in a cone of damp newspaper and fragile ones inside plastic bags. Keep them out of sunlight, which quickly dehydrates these delicate beauties once they are cut.

Forcing flowers

In late winter, lovely blossoming branches of forsythia, apple, quince, prunus and flowering currant can be forced into early opening very easily, as can horse chestnut, willow, hazel, and whitebeam foliage. Cut when you see the buds starting to plump up. Flower buds are often round in shape, leaf buds more pointed. Bring them into the warmth of the house and hammer the stem ends. Let them drink in a few inches of boiling water in a jug or bucket; when this has cooled, top up with warm water and leave it in a warm, light place, and the buds will slowly open. Or you can arrange the branches at once in a container of very hot water and await the little miracle. Florists' gladioli and roses are among the flowers which can be forced in a similar way at any time of year, though care should be taken not to allow steam to damage the flowerheads.

Retarding flowers

It is sickening when something is in perfect flower but you don't actually want to use it in an arrangement until a special occasion the next week! Many subjects can be retarded if picked while still in close bud and

brought into a cool dark place. Wrap them in newspaper and leave them in a bucket of cool water until required.

Gladioli and peonies will keep out of water for some days on the cold concrete floor of a garage. It is also possible to retard flowers in a refrigerator set no colder than 5.5 degrees Centigrade. First give the blooms a good drink, dry the stalks, then seal them, stems and all, into kitchen foil or polythene. This is a trick more and more florists are using, but the life-span of flowers treated in this manner may be very much reduced.

Aftercare

Once arranged, all fresh plant materials need a constant source of moisture. If they are allowed to dry out completely many never fully recover. Every couple of days renew the water in containers, using fresh, tepid (not icy-cold) water, or keep the level topped up. Keep soaked foam consistently damp — a small watering-can with a long, thin spout is useful. Splashes and spills are less likely if the foam is supported in a saucer-shaped holder, or if there is a convenient gap between foam and container. In hot weather, use a fine atomizer to spray flowers and foliage with water at room temperature, so that it can be absorbed through the petals and leaves. Flowers with fleshy petals, such as lilies and alstroemeria, may take exception to this rule and come out in brown spots!

Move an arrangement from a precious surface to a wipe-clean worktop when you are watering or spraying it, and do not replace it until water has stopped dripping from the leaves or flowerheads.

Try to place a fresh flower arrangement in a cool situation away from strong light, direct heat or draughts which (perhaps surprisingly) cause severe dehydration. Central heating, open fires and fumes from oil- or other stoves, all have a bad effect on fresh materials. At night, move an arrangement from a room with an all-night fire or burner to a cooler spot — perhaps an unheated spare bedroom — if possible.

Cut off dead flower heads regularly, snip off any wilting or tired-looking leaves and replace them with fresh ones which have been properly conditioned. By a little judicious substitution you can keep an arrangement looking at its peak for much longer.

Proprietary brands of cut flower food are also available to help prolong the life of cut flowers.

A tightly-closed red rosebud is appealing in the mysterious, romantic depth of its colour; a pale pink dogrose from the hedgerows because of the clear innocence of its soft tints; a cluster of Masquerade roses for the vibrant juxtaposition of pink, scarlet and yellow. A rose is a rose is a rose, but by its colour a flower can suggest a variety of moods and appeal to each of us for different reasons. All sorts of colours can look their best against differing backgrounds in the home.

Colour is so much a matter of personal choice that when you arrange flowers there are no really hard-and-fast rules, no right and wrong. However, a basic appreciation of the quality and balance of colour can help you achieve flower groupings that are a pleasure to look at, creating just the effect you intend.

According to the colours you choose, a flower arrangement can appear to bring warmth or coolness to a room; may seem close or splendidly isolated; can show up well in poor light; may display a study in monochrome or span all the hues of a rainbow.

Red and orange bring a warm glow on a cold day — a bowl of coral dahlias, ruby chrysanthemums and orange rosehips can be as welcoming as a log fire — while arrangements of mainly blue and green flowers and foliage, ice-cool colours, provide a contrast to the heat of summer. Violet and yellow take their cue from neighbouring colours and tend to look warm against red and orange or cool with blue and green.

In a very small room, a predominantly red and orange arrangement may give the illusion of crowding, for these colours seem to come forward towards the viewer; whereas green, blue and violet are termed receding colours, which can create a feeling of space.

The strength and type of lighting in the room has an important bearing on your choice of plant material. When the light is poor, as it might be in a narrow hall, a room corner or a church, choose light, bright colours, such as yellow and white flowers, or the palest tints of blue, red and orange, with yellow and lime green foliage rather than heavy blue-green shades which might fade into the background. If, on the other hand, an arrangement is particularly well lighted — under a strip light in an alcove or by a directional spotlight — pale yellow and white flowers can look washed out.

Colours go full circle

Colours are divided naturally into six groups or families — 'naturally' meaning the way they are seen in a rainbow, with red at the top. The three main families are the pure, primary colours of red, blue and yellow. The other three are between these hues; violet, which is a mixture of red and blue; green, composed of blue and yellow; and orange, which is made up of yellow and red. The relationships of these colours can be seen on the Colour Wheel (left) — those which are next to each other, and called adjacent, those that are opposite each other, and called complementary and those that alternate around the wheel, and are called triadic.

Apart from these six colours, or hues, there are white, black and grey, referred to as neutrals. And, of course, all the varying tonal intensities of the six colours. When white is mixed with a colour, red for example, the resulting pale red, or pink, is called a tint. When black is mixed with it, darkening the colour intensity, it is called a shade (a deep shade of red) and when grey is mixed with a hue, it becomes a tone.

To get used to mixing and matching colours it is a useful idea to cut out paint and fabric samples and move them around, putting related colours close together, then opposites; all pale tints, all dark shades and so on, and noting which combinations you find most attractive and which look best in your home. You will soon instinctively be able to translate this experience into your flower groupings.

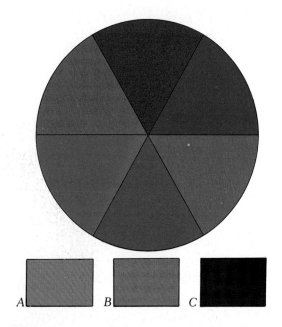

A colour wheel composed of primary and secondary hues. The addition of white (A), grey (B) and black (C) to red produces the tint, tone and shade of that colour.

When you blend a variety of colours, arrange the strongest shade with a firm hand — notice how the red pyrethrums make a lazy S shape through this design.

A single colour offset with white can create a striking effect. Here sprays of lilac give visual weight to the design, which is completed with translucent clusters of cranesbill.

Subtle tints of yellow, orange and red, next to each other on the colour wheel, make a harmonious choice for a collection of summer flowers. Blue, purple and red, also adjacent to each other, are equally harmonious yet bold in flower arrangements.

The thick, waxy petals of alstroemeria have a cooling effect, even in tints of red and yellow. Ice-green lamium leaves complete the display. This is an example of using triadic colours, that is those which alternate around the colour wheel.

Red and green are on opposite sides of the colour wheel and are perfectly complementary against a neutral background.

Bluebells curving gently in the wind; the sharp angles of a branch silhouetted against the sky; a prize delphinium, most stately of stems, standing rigidly to attention — the lines and curves of plants as they grow are important characteristics. Equally, in arranging plant materials to decorate the home or for a special occasion, these same shapes, some gracefully flowing and some angular, are the key to pleasing designs with a natural appearance.

What is considered good design in flower arranging — as it is in art and architecture — is largely a matter of proportion and balance. If these are well-realized, then arranged flowers can look just as fine and natural as when they are growing.

Of course, it is possible simply to drop a bunch of flowers into a favourite container — tall red poppies in a slender *art nouveau* pot, perhaps — and create a delightful effect. But floral art has more to offer than that. With a little understanding of the design principles that form the basis of all advanced and competitive work, you can greatly increase your enjoyment and the scope of your arrangements.

A sense of proportion

Before you decide on the shape of an arrangement, consider where it is to be placed. The situation may impose certain disciplines or suggest the shape that will look most effective. For a dining-table you may want a low, horizontal design; for an alcove, one that is long and slender or forms a right-angle around the frame; for a table against a wall, a display with generous height and width; and so on. Then choose a suitable container, one that will hold the plant material adequately, is the right colour and, just as important, the correct proportion.

It is generally considered that in formal flower arrangements, whether they are horizontal, upright or triangular, the length of the most extended stem (or stems) should be at least one and a half times the width or height of the container.

For example if you wish to use a shallow baking dish on a wooden base 20cm (8 in) wide for a low, flat arrangement, then each side stem, whether they are budding roses or branches of foliage, should be at least 30cm (12 in) long. Similarly, if you want to create an upright design 45cm (18 in) high, perhaps to fit a niche, then your container should represent no more than 30cm (12 in) of the total height. Until you are practised enough to judge the proportion by eye, it is advisable to measure the container and the length of stems before you cut them.

These main stems, which establish the proportion, should be put in position first and the rest of the stems placed so that they appear to flow naturally and easily from them. The height of a horizontal design, the width of a vertical one or the spread of a symmetrical or equal-sided triangle shape can all be variable. Using the same shallow container and long, flowing side stems it is possible to create a very low design for a table centre or one that extends upwards, perhaps for a sideboard or church window, and all will be in perfect proportion.

Graduation — the easy way

For the most natural effect, flowers and foliage should be arranged so that the largest blooms and heaviest leaves are positioned at the base, and the smallest flowers or buds and the most slender stems at the top and side tips. The reason for this is clear — that is how they grow. Take, for example, a stem of delphinium. The fully-opened flowers are at the base, the partly-opened ones above them, graduating to the tightly-closed buds at the tip. Follow the same sequence with foliage, placing heavy leaves such as helleborus and fig at the base, for visual weight, moving through medium-sized leaves to fine ones, such as berberis and privet, at the tips.

The focus of attention

The correct use of graduating materials makes any design literally easy on the eye. Quite naturally, and without any effort, the eye travels from the fine tip of the display, through the middle range to the centre — and there it pauses. This is known as the focal point of the design, and should be carefully planned to create impact. At this point — the right angle of an L-shape, the centre of a Hogarth curve or crescent, the centre base of a horizontal, and always at the base of the main stem — you should place your choicest material. This will vary according to the design and may be a trio of the largest, darkest and most perfect flowers, a cluster of glistening red berries, a single eye-catching bloom or a beautiful variegated and shiny leaf.

The discipline of a symmetrical triangle makes this a simple shape for beginners to achieve. Rose hips, ivy, periwinkle and lamium leaves define the points and cream spray carnations fill in the design.

An asymmetrical display of peonies, geraniums, sweet peas, wild and cultivated roses, nepita and columbine skilfully avoids the deadening effect which can be the result of pure symmetry.

When you want an arrangement that will not obscure the view or block the light, on a dining table or in a window, a low horizontal display, such as the one above, is ideal. Yellow and white marguerites catch every ray of pale sunlight.

Sweet peas and clematis foliage, left, stem from a block of foam held in a bottle lid, fitted to the neck of the container. The flowers and foliage form a 'lazy S', or Hogarth curve.

The angular lines of the rosewood tea caddy, above, suggest a geometric arrangement. The L-shape is achieved with spring flowers and deep green helleborus leaves.

THE PROMISE OF SPRING

CATKINS

DAFFODIL

PHEASANT'S
EYE NARCISSUS

MAHONIA FLOWER

GRAPE
HYACINTH

NARCISSUS
'CHEERFULNESS'

PUSSY WILLOW

FORGET-ME-NOT

ANEMONE

TULIP

HYACINTH

HEBE FOLIAGE

DOUBLE
SNOWDROP

A brief study of the theory of colour and proportion, illustrated on the preceding pages, will help you appreciate the thought that has gone into the natural-looking, seasonal arrangements which follow.

In the windowsill design (opposite) the spring flowers fan out like clear, pale rays of sunshine. The deeper colours — dark mauve anemones, grape hyacinths and forget-me-nots — are clustered close together around the rim of the container, a flower-patterned vegetable dish. The design spreads outwards at the top with flowers of lighter colours, to avoid a top-heavy effect and the outline is delicately extended with foliage.

ROSES, ROSES ALL THE WAY

NATURALLY BEAUTIFUL

During the summer, when so many beautiful flowers fill our gardens and are available from every flower shop and stall, it is almost impossible to choose favourites. Whether your preference is for an old-fashioned garden full of scented roses and tumbling herbs, or a meadow splashed with the bright colours of buttercups, daisies, poppies and cornflowers, we have tried to cater for it.

Incidentally, it is worth noting, before you set off to collect armfuls of wild flowers from the countryside, that certain plants (such as the cowslip) are protected and should not be picked, if future generations are to enjoy them. If you live in the country, native plants may seed themselves naturally in a domestic garden. Otherwise, seeds of wild flowers are now available from many specialist seed suppliers and nurseries.

In the conservatory (opposite) there's a basket of full-blown, headily-scented roses arranged just as they grow — casually, naturally, and tumbling together — with trails of variegated ivy curving over the basket.

To make the roses last longer, remember to crush the stem ends lightly, or split them with a sharp knife; in hot, humid weather, spray the flowers with tepid water from a fine-mist atomiser.

In quite a different mood, but equally informal, the pottery basket (above) is filled with buttercups and daisies. Notice that some of the golden petals have dropped, leaving the large, domed yellow centres, attractive in themselves.

Baskets and other wide-necked containers can make even a casual arrangement difficult as the flowers have no means of support. However, concealed crumpled wire netting (see page 105) discreetly solves the problem and tames the stems in the inner container.

ALSTROEMERIA

GLYCERINED
BEECH LEAVES

GLYCERINED
MAHONIA LEAVES

DRIED ASPIDISTRA

SPRAY
CHRYSANTHEMUMS

GLYCERINED
BLACKBERRY LEAVES

IVY

CHINESE LANTERNS

ROSES

This glorious study of autumn shades consists of a selection of seasonal garden flowers blended with dried and glycerine-preserved material. As the flowers fade and die they can be replaced by fresh blooms, while the backbone of the arrangement remains the same.

The ingredients used here consist of a 'skeleton' of glycerined mahonia leaves, which have an almost sculptural quality, and sprays of glycerined blackberry leaves and beech leaves, in their well known deep, coppery colour. In addition the shapely curves of dried leaves of aspidistra give movement to the design, while dried Chinese lanterns have been cut and opened out to make interesting and varied flower shapes (see page 83) revealing the heavy central fruits.

Freshness is provided by foliage in the form of ivy in varying shapes and sizes — sprays with large, dark berries and others providing a slender trail of heavily-veined leaves. The floral contribution is made up of

bronze 'spider' chrysanthemums, apricot and pale bronze single spray chrysanthemums with brilliant gold centres, some individual flowers of bright coral alstroemeria which have been cut and inserted close to the holding foam, and late-flowering pale peach and apricot roses selected to team with the colours of the spray chrysanthemums. Information on the use and positioning of holding foam is given on page 104.

The whole arrangement, and variations on it, would give warmth and vibrancy to the dullest of winter days. Both roses and chrysanthemums are relatively long-lived in arrangements, but as you come to replace fading flowers, consider introducing a different colour emphasis. Keep to warm tones, but substitute peachy-pink for apricot roses, deep red for coral chrysanthemums. The colours of autumn flowers are subtle and naturally harmonious. For a more striking variation, choose brighter shades of gold, yellow and rich cream.

THE LAST ROSE OF SUMMER

FLOWERS FOR THE HOME

*E*veryone has favourite flowers and preferences as to the shape and colour, and in many cases the scent, of particular flower types. But while it is delightful to fill a room with the presence of roses, spring flowers or chrysanthemums, perhaps you tend always to choose the same things? Or you may feel, as many people do, that you lack the extra spark of inspiration that produces something really unusual and individual? Just look around your home and you will find a wealth of colour cues and settings with a specific mood, little niches, shelves or pieces of furniture, or a familiar picture, that seem admirably suited to a specially designed flower arrangement. Pick up these cues and make them the basis of your flower choices.

The overall colour scheme of a large living room or guest bedroom will readily suggest ideas for flowers. Don't neglect the kitchen, especially if you spend most of your time there working, or the bathroom where you may have time to relax. Whether your taste is for the traditional, or you have austere modern furnishings with clean lines and colours, we provide suggestions that will complement almost any style and setting.

Traditional chintz curtain fabric, a modern abstract print, an Oriental screen, a complete scheme in black and white — your furnishings and accessories can spark off ideas for flower arrangements that are entirely individual and complementary. Flowers can not only capture the mood or atmosphere or a room, they can draw attention to a special piece of furniture, conceal a low-key feature such as an empty fireplace or dreary view, or be as pretty as a picture on a blank wall.

Certain flowers and ways of arranging them are associated with particular furnishing styles. A comfortable country home with chintz curtains, deep sofas and a restful air is the perfect setting for large bowls of voluptuous flowers such as roses, peonies, hydrangeas, foxgloves and hollyhocks. A symmetrical design (see page 19) would be perfect in summer, and the country display opposite is a delightful herald of autumn — the copper can, with its roses, rosehips, berries and grapes, catches every dancing glint of firelight.

In a country cottage, or even a town flat where the owner has attempted to give the impression of being surrounded by birds and trees, wild flowers and tumbling garden flowers are natural choices. If you have wallpaper and curtains with small floral patterns, resist the temptation to echo them exactly in the flowers, or you will need a searchlight to see them. Pick up the colour of the furnishings in larger flowers, or choose much darker shades or a complete contrast. Baskets, porcelain, blue and white pottery and sparkling white ornaments are ideal containers.

When the birds and trees in your furnishings and accessories evoke not the British countryside but an Oriental flavour, take your cue for complementary designs using twigs, blossoms and few, if any, flowers (see page 34).

Sparse use of flowers seems appropriate, too, in settings of a completely different kind — rooms furnished in 'high tech' style, with black and white contrasts, chrome, plastic, glass and stainless steel predominating. Choosing these uncompromising materials does not mean that flowers are out of place. See how we meet the challenge on page 33.

Kitchens and bathrooms

Many kitchens and bathrooms need flowers and plants to soften their appearance. It makes it seem much less arduous to be slaving over a hot stove, much more

relaxing to soak quietly in the bath, if there is a nosegay of flowers to enjoy.

For rooms with a hot and steamy atmosphere, choose tough flowers that can withstand heat and humidity, or go for here-today-and-gone-tomorrow bunches of flowers casually placed in a simple container. The arrangement of single chrysanthemums, alstroemeria, carnations and roses shown on page 36 would bring a luxurious and romantic look to a large country bathroom — would you ever want to leave it?

In the kitchen, where flowers tend to have a short shelf life, time-consuming arrangements are not usually in order. For a country look, a honey jar of herbs, garden and wild flowers is pretty and practical — there's always a sprig of parsley or mint to hand.

Genuine reproductions

A painting or print can provide the key to flower arrangements in perfect harmony. The colours in an abstract painting can be stunningly repeated in a bowl of floating flowerheads beneath it. A print of a Dutch Old Master flower painting can inspire a copy of the style in a jug of mixed flowers with multiple colours and infinite detail, or a cornfield scene may be complemented by a cider jar brimming over with wheat, oats, cornflowers and poppies.

Everyone has at least one or two treasured pieces of furniture, an heirloom, a wedding present or a bargain hard-won in a sale room, perhaps. Let them take centre stage to increase the impact of your flower arrangements, never relegate them to a role just as flower stands. A dressing-table with a mirror can reflect two designs for the price of one (remember to make your flower displays as neat at the back as at the front!); a polished writing table can attract admiring glances beckoned by a posy in a pewter ink stand; and a Victorian whatnot is just the thing for sugar-candy colours and trails of ivy.

Place a long, low arrangement of flowers on a windowsill as a half-way stage between home and garden, or increase the height of the display if the view is best ignored. In summer, fill a lonely fireplace with dancing-flame colours — zinneas, dahlias, rudbeckias — and it can still be the focal point of the room.

By the careful choice of flowers you can enhance every room and make working and relaxing at home all the more enjoyable, a reward well worth a little effort.

THE FRUITS OF THE COUNTRY

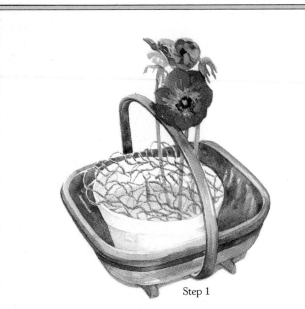

Step 1

The restful, soothing effect of flowers is particularly apparent in a bedroom. Make it a rule to pamper yourself with a small nosegay, always in fresh water, on your dressing-table or by your bedside, and be sure to offer guests this most flattering token of welcome.

Pretty ceramic containers, especially those with floral designs, figurines and small junk-shop finds of silver or glassware, all have the homely touch suitable for a country cottage bedroom.

Baskets are also a good choice. Particularly pretty are those spray-painted in pastel colours — pale green, pink or cream — to team with spriggy wallpaper or a treasured quilt. A round squat basket of roses in front of a small black fireplace, a long narrow arrangement on a windowsill, a handled basket hanging in a ceiling corner, a tiny posy-basket on a chest or dressing-table — these are all the stuff that dreams are made of.

A basket of flowers

This pretty arrangement for a bedroom (right) is a small, square willow trug filled to overflowing with anemones and snowdrops.

Step 2

Step 1 Place an inner bowl inside the trug. Cut a piece of 5-cm (2-in) wire netting measuring about 27cm (18 in) square. Crush it in your hands and place it in the bowl so that it extends just above the rim of the trug. Partly fill the container with water. Place three tall anemones in the centre.
Step 2 Cut the stems of the others in graded heights. Insert them so that the shortest stems are closest to the rim to make a 'cushion' effect.
Step 3 Insert long trails of variegated ivy at one side and single leaves amongst the anemones. Place snow-drops at random, clustering three or four together to avoid a spotted appearance.

Step 3

A BASKET OF FLOWERS

Styles of interior design are continually changing; floral art is equally adaptable and can be used to reflect the character of each new idea. Nothing would be more incongruous than a chrome and glass dining table adorned with a fussy porcelain teapot pouring out a froth of blowsy flowers. But nothing seems more lonely than an austerely furnished room without a single flower or plant in sight.

Colour and texture play a particularly important part in modern furnishings of all kinds, and these can be reflected accurately and appropriately in the choice of plant materials.

Monochromatic schemes

Rooms furnished in the Scandinavian style, with white walls and cream or grey furnishing, are marvellous settings for huge stone jars crammed with flowers of a single type. White marguerites have acquired a classic status. White or palest lemon single chrysanthemums, white primulas, geraniums, campanula or antirrhinums, arranged in hand-thrown pots or wooden containers, are striking alternatives. Large plants such as aspidistra, philodendron and weeping fig, standing on the floor in basket-weave jardinières, are another way to introduce a splash of living colour with an acceptable degree of restraint.

Picking up textures

Any room in which texture is a vital feature is tailor-made for flower designs developed around natural materials gathered from the woodland or seashore. Driftwood might well have been the initial inspiration for rough-textured carpets and fabrics, and is dramatic as a background for two or three elegant flowers — Easter lilies or crown imperials — or a single ornamental cabbage, for example. A shallow dish of seaworn pebbles can conceal a pinholder and support a few stark stems of poppy or onion seedheads, or a single large thistle or globe artichoke head.

The traditional rules of flower arranging (see page 18), do not apply, of course, to modern and free interpretations. Aim to maintain a visual balance, but let your design respond to the natural shapes — of bleached wood, twigs, branches, twisted leaves — and even exaggerate them. (As with modern furnishings, so with flower arranging; avoid at all costs a cluttered or confused look. Better a single flower seen in all its glory than a clump of six that look like a ball of knitting!)

Contrast shiny natural materials — granite, shells — with dull-surfaced flowers and leaves and vice-versa. This mix-and-match of gloss against matt surfaces, those which catch the light contrasted with others that don't, keeps design interest alive.

You can bring a greater range of metallic glints to a high-tech room by spraying flowers and foliage with aerosol cans of silver or gold paint — bronze and copper are also available, but they are less effective. Choose leaves with clearly defined, spiky shapes. Mahonia, yucca, thistle and holly are good candidates.

Spraying is a way of both gilding flowers and preserving them. A rose may be considered out of place in an uncompromisingly modern room but a silver rose — that's another matter. Try spraying gladioli, irises, tree peonies and Enchantment lilies too — since it makes the flowers virtually everlasting, even the most expensive varieties become economical. (Instructions for spraying plant materials are on page 56.)

Tune in to high tech

Now that we have reached the technological age, and the focal point of a living room is likely to be a sophisticated electronic masterpiece, there's scope for another style of floral art. This is no place for sentiment and it takes flowers and foliage with a wax-like, almost haughty, characteristic to match the tone. Arum and other lilies, magnolias, camellias, tulips, hosta, Solomon's seal and onopordum leaves, cool and self-sufficient, can hold their own.

Nor is there a place here for modest containers. Look for sculptured glass, rectangular glass fish tanks, speckled black enamel urns, black glazed pottery, small, shiny galvanised buckets. Explore new sources for objects to suit new styles.

Cocktail time!

For a room all set for glittering cocktail time (opposite), our choice is a heavy glass container of architectural proportions and five simple stems of Madonna lilies. The clean lines are created by stripping the leaves from the lower stems to draw attention to the sparkling glass. To prolong the life of the lilies, cut the flowers off as they fade and slightly shorten the stems.

COCKTAIL TIME

EASTERN MAGIC

A red-lacquered box or chest, a rice-paper lantern, a bamboo screen, a beautiful Chinese porcelain bowl — a single item is enough to inspire you to look East for ideas about flowers and assemble an Oriental corner.

Ikebana, the Japanese floral art, dates from the sixth century when Buddhism was introduced to the nation and the priests arranged flowers to decorate the temples. This dignified and elegant art form is a study in itself. Each item of plant material, the way it is placed and the direction it faces has a deep significance impossible to appreciate without careful research. What is immediately discernible to Western eyes is the restraint exercised. The very word Ikebana means the 'way' or direction of flowers, and the philosophical aim of the art is the attainment of supreme beauty using the minimum amount of plant material. Without the necessary study, we can only emulate the simplicity.

Among your collection of containers you will almost certainly have one or two that are suitable for Oriental-style arrangements. Shallow containers such as pottery fruit bowls or dark-coloured rectangular baking dishes, flat items like bamboo place mats or a wooden bread-board are all suitable. Modern pottery vases with their clean, uncluttered lines are the right style for upright displays.

In oriental designs twigs play an important role — in Ikebana a function of stems is to create strong directional lines representing heaven, earth and man —

and flowers are used sparingly, if at all. Typical groupings could be a pottery plate with pussy willow, magnolia leaves and three lilies held by a concealed pinholder; a tall, cylindrical stone pot with curving sprays of spotted laurel and five long-stemmed carnations, or a brass urn supporting three well-shaped stems of cherry blossom.

Eastern magic

The container is a classic, beautifully proportioned stone pot, an ideal visual contrast to the twisting, angular lines of fruit blossom twigs. Five single white chrysanthemums clustered around the base demonstrate the spellbinding effect that can be achieved with a minimum of materials.

Step 1 Place a pinholder in the base of the pot. Lower it in carefully — dropping the heavy metal onto the stone could prove disastrous. Select stems of fruit blossom with pleasing curves and try them for size in the pot.
Step 2 Cut the chosen stems to the required length. Lightly crush the stem ends, using a mallet or hammer. This enables the woody stems to take up water more easily.
Step 3 Arrange the twigs of blossom, pushing them firmly on to the pinholder. Arrange the chrysanthemum stems, using the twigs as a 'barrier', to keep them in place.

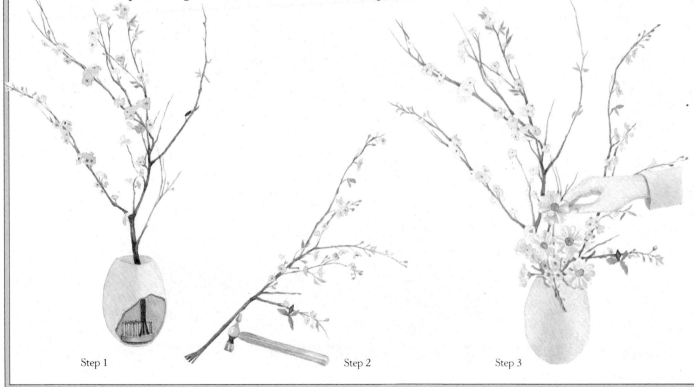

Step 1   Step 2   Step 3

JUG AND BOWL ENSEMBLE

A tall, white, water jug, overflowing with sunrise-coloured flowers, and a wash basin decorated with a summer posy — either design would be charming by itself; together they more than double the impact.

It is often possible to use matching containers in eye-catching ways, to create extra height or width, fill an awkward corner or hold different kinds of flowers. For a unified effect, link the containers visually by your choice of plant materials, with trailing foliage or a stray bud carrying the eye from one to the other, or by placing them so that they slightly overlap.

A scaled-down version of this washstand group could be made in a pretty cup and saucer. A milk jug and sugar bowl or a gravy boat and stand also have potential. Make use of harmonious but bright colours.

One at a time

Make each item of the arrangement separately: arrange the flowers in the jug first and then tuck in the rest of the materials around it. Here's how it's done.

Condition all the flowers and foliage (see page 13). Soak a large block and a small cylinder of water-retaining foam. Wedge the block of foam in the jug to extend about 7.5cm (3 in) above the rim. Cover it with crumpled wire netting (see page 104) and wire this securely to the handle.

The choice of plant materials for the jug is single spray chrysanthemums in two shades of coral, alstroemerias speckled with deep bronze, two-tone coral carnations, pink roses, sprays of ivy with black berries, trails of variegated ivy leaves tinged with pink, and carnation leaves. To decorate the bowl there are carnations, cream and pink roses, white spray chrysanthemums, sage, wallflower and ivy leaves.

The jug

Stand the jug in the bowl.
Step 1 Position the side trails of ivy, the tall central carnation buds, roses and alstroemeria, and the alstroemeria on both sides.
Step 2 Place alstroemeria in a staggered line down the centre front.
Step 3 Fill in with spray chrysanthemums in graduated heights.
Step 4 Fill in with carnations, roses and ivy leaves.
Step 5 Cover all traces of holding material with short sprays of leaves.

Step 1

Steps 2 and 3

Steps 4 and 5

Step 1

Step 2

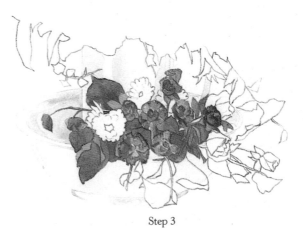

Step 3

Slice the soaked foam cylinder in half downwards and wrap it in foil. Tape this section to the inside of the bowl so it extends 5cm (2 in) above the rim.

The flowers that decorate the bowl are chosen to match or echo the shapes and colours in the jug arrangement. These are carnations, cream and pink roses, white spray chrysanthemums, sage, wallflower and ivy leaves. The white and cream flowers lift the tone, drawing the posy out from the shadow of the larger group. The sage and wallflower leaves repeat the larger shapes, with a slight variation of tone and texture. The ivy is again tinged with pink; its trailing habit forms a natural link between the two elements of the design.

The posy is designed to complement the flowers in the jug, not to compete with them. Stand back from the work from time to time to check the overall effect.

The bowl

Step 1 Position two sprays of ivy and the rose buds diagonally.
Step 2 Place the arc of white chrysanthemums.
Step 3 Fill in the centre with carnations and cover the holding material with leaves.

Low pieces of furniture, such as coffee tables, are often adorned with flowers because they are vacant and conveniently distant from hobby and work areas. But your problem might be that there is not a square centimetre of space where you can position a few flowers. One solution is to make use of wall space with specially designed hanging wall vases.

Taking a bird's eye view

Low coffee tables are virtually unique in that they are almost always viewed from above. Such flower arrangements must be worked with this viewpoint constantly in mind, so that they look attractive from every angle.

A variety of objects can be turned to good account as containers, such as cigarette or trinket boxes, shallow wicker baskets or ceramic imitations, flat dishes and bowls. For your peace of mind, the container should be reasonably low and equipped with a firm base.

Viewed from above, every table top has a geometric shape and it is interesting to follow this in the flower design. Using purpose-made foam holders, or improvising for yourself, you can build a design that forms a crescent or a complete hoop to nestle close to the edge of a circular table; an L-shape echoing the proportions of a square or rectangle, or even an ambitious six-sided display for a hexagonal surface.

The plant material should fit quite tightly within an overall outline, which means cutting stems very short and pressing the flowers and leaves close to the foam.

To make a shaped foam base, cut blocks of foam about 5cm (2 in) deep, 5cm (2 in) wide and the required length. To achieve the curve in a circle or crescent, they should be no more than 7.5cm (3 in) long. Trim the corners to fit, if necessary. Soak the foam, wrap it in strips of foil about 22.5cm (9 in) wide and mould it gently in your hands to perfect the shape. Make holes through the foil with a wooden cocktail stick when inserting slender stems.

Wall-flowers

There are many situations, for example in narrow halls, small kitchens and bathrooms, where hanging flowers on the wall is the only way to introduce them at all. Even in large, more generously furnished rooms, a flower arrangement can be just what is needed to 'lift' a blank wall, link two or more pictures into a unified

group or provide a focal point where one is lacking.

The principles are the same whether you choose a thirties-style wall vase in pink or pearly ceramic glaze or a modern pottery vase in earthy colours. According to the shape and the angle of the vase against the wall, you can opt for a trailing, 'hanging-basket' effect with slender tendrils of, say, everlasting pea and clematis, or go for a cornucopia, or 'horn of plenty', effect. This look can be carried out with small, compact flower heads close to the container graduating to large, full blooms at the extent of the design.

For trouble-free fillers that need little maintenance, you can plant a wall vase with vigorous trailing plants like 'mind your own business' or busy Lizzie, or make a display of dried flowers, cereals and grasses.

In the design (above) the mood of the beautiful thirties-style plates has been reflected in the flowers. The palest of pink roses and white, pink and creamy-green ranunculus have been used, with pride of place going to a sparkling fully-open yellow bloom. The foliage is variegated periwinkle leaves and small-leaved trailing ivy.

With all arrangements in wall vases it is a good idea to lift the vase from the wall and stand it upright in a jug or bowl while you arrange or water the flowers.

FLOWERS FOR SPECIAL OCCASIONS

*H*ave *you ever seen a wedding without flowers? They are an indispensable part of the happiest occasions in our lives, one of the first items to be planned for a large or formal reception, and a very public expression of celebration. But there are many more private and individual occasions, when formality is out of place, that can be marked as special by the thoughtful provision of a simple posy or nosegay.*

Flowers and food are natural partners, from an elegant centrepiece for a dinner table to a pretty flower garnish for a single dish. Informal buffets are cheered by the presence of flowers, and you can arrange them with fruit, vegetables or pulses to catch the flavour of the buffet menu. Make good use of foliage, choosing unexpected colours and textures or highly decorative variegations. At Christmas, evergreens form a seasonal background for a vivid display of fresh flowers, or of plant materials sprayed in festive colours.

It is almost impossible to imagine preparing for a special family occasion, celebrating a religious festival or giving a party without posies, nosegays, garlands, swags, baskets and arrangements of flowers. Whether you want to set the scene for a merry Christmas and a happy New Year, surprise a loved one or guest with breakfast in bed, give a party indoors or in the garden, send off the bridal couple in a waft of joy or celebrate fifty golden years — flowers should be there.

Natural partners

Flowers and food have a special affinity. The prettiest china we choose when entertaining friends is often garlanded with flowers; how many of the beautiful still life paintings we admire are a perfect harmony of fruit, vegetables and flowers.

It is not necessary to go to great lengths to create an impact. Decorating food with flowers and leaves can be less time-consuming than piping cream or cutting crudités, and displaying one or two perfect blooms in a wine glass at each place setting or floating a few flowerheads in water, takes only moments.

The selection of the container and the colour and type of flowers is all-important. You are halfway there if your initial choices are suitable for the occasion.

When you are setting a table or tray, spare items of the tableware make perfect containers — for example, a small casserole or two or three egg cups. Otherwise, match your container to the *mood* as well as the colour of the set, choosing china, silver, bronze or glass for a formal design and wood, hand-thrown pottery, rush or canework for a rustic look.

Take practical considerations into account. Flowers for a dinner party should be low enough to enable guests to see each other — and the food — easily. For a buffet party, a tall, eye-catching design is certainly suitable. It need not be elaborate. An elegant table centre of orchids, magnolias and lilies could be as out of place at a spaghetti supper as a ballgown at a barbecue. Containers with natural pedestals, such as cake stands, ham stands and tall urns, are ideal.

Milestones in colour

The occasion itself often gives a lead in the choice of colour. Flowers for a christening party can be pink and cream tulips, roses or dahlias, according to season, or choose blue irises, cornflowers and alkanet. If you're stumped for blue flowers, you can create your own by standing the stems of white blooms in a pot of ink. As the stems take up the liquid the flowers change colour.

Silver weddings call for beautiful foliage such as rosemary, onopordum, hosta and ballota to highlight white and off-white flowers, delicately tinged with yellow, pink, blue or green. Golden wedding party flowers are plentiful all year round. Blend yellow with pale shades of cream, tinged with blue or green, for delicate contrast.

For emphasis, spray some foliage with gold paint, following the method on page 56. As a keepsake of the occasion you could present the 'silver' or 'golden' wife, with some flowers from the arrangement preserved for ever by metallic spray paint.

Every season will give you a generous selection of flowers for a ruby wedding. Harmonize the many tones of red that you find in gladioli, zinnias, hibiscus, rhododendron. And note that the soft greens of tobacco plants, hellebores, *Alchemilla mollis* and euphorbia are more delightful complements to red than the strong contrast of white flowers.

A good send-off

Flowers for a wedding will be designed around the bride's choice of colour scheme — this can be carried out in the bouquets and in the church and reception room. If the cake is displayed on a separate table, to be whisked backstage for cutting, a flower arrangement will be the centrepiece of the top table. For a sit-down meal, the flowers must be low in front of the bridal couple, but for a buffet a gloriously tall display, a profusion of the most romantic flowers, is in order. Follow the instructions for a table pedestal on page 79 and a floral swag for the top table on page 54.

When Christmas comes

Floral swags, so elegantly simple, enter into all kinds of celebrations and can be draped in all manner of places — to outline the entrance to a marquee for a summer dance, to brighten a doorway or porch, to loop down a stairway or — at Christmas time — over the fireplace. Instead of garnishing a holly and ivy swag with flowers and berries, wire it with tiny dessert apples, cooking pears, nuts and clementines for an unusually festive air.

Step 1

Step 2

Dusk falls, the candles are flickering and in a few moments your table will be the centre of attention. To suit the occasion, we have designed an arrangement that is casual in style but unashamedly dramatic.

This is a mirror-image design, worked first on one side and then the reverse, to be equally attractive from all angles. Divide your flowers and foliage into two more or less equal groups, so that when you have completed the front you have a matching selection for the back. The container is a shallow pottery vegetable dish, the holding material a block of foam extending just above the rim.

A dinner table arrangement

Cut the foam and hold it in place with a piece of string tied to the handles of the dish.

Step 1 Cut matching sprays of camellia foliage, or other stems that curve to both right and left so that they are complementary when placed back to back. Position the sprays that define the full height and width at each side, and place two short sprays at the front.
Step 2 Arrange white anemones in an arc from side to side, then position others above and below them.
Step 3 Place mauve anemones, taking care that some break over the rim of the dish. Cut a few stems really short and push them close to the foam, to conceal it.
Step 4 Strip away fuchsia leaves and insert the flower stems between the anemones. Fill in spaces with short sprays of foliage.

Reverse the design and repeat on the other side.

Step 3

Step 4

Flowers and food go together in the simplest and most decorative ways. Give the personal touch to a place setting, garnish a tasty dish with morsels of bright colour, or make a feature of edible flowers and leaves.

Add a sprig of mint, borage or lemon verbena to cool summer drinks or cocktails, or freeze the leaves or flowers inside ice cubes. Marigold or nasturtium petals are both colourful and palatable in salads, and borage or bergamot leaves provide delicate flavour. In cooking, use herbs both to flavour and embellish sauces or dressings, or include peppery capers, which are actually unopened flower buds. Flowers can even become the main course — courgette flowers filled with a savoury vegetable stuffing.

Crystallized flowers are pretty decoration for cakes and puddings — violets, rose petals, the flowers of versatile borage, or candied angelica stems. Buy crystallized blooms or make your own by brushing the flowers with egg white and dusting on caster sugar. Leave the flowers covered and in a cool place until they are dry. Store in an airtight container.

The six ideas shown here make considerable impact, but each is simple and takes only moments of your time. So little effort is needed to give a special, memorable appearance to your lunch or dinner table.

Cool green and cream; scented pelargonium leaves team tastefully with a dish of vanilla ice cream. And you can eat the leaves!

The Oriental way with flowers is to float one or two perfect blooms in a bowl of water. Spider chrysanthemums are often used in this way in Chinese and Japanese floral art.

Marigold petals are delicious and add a dash of brilliant colour to an endive and watercress salad.

Just a couple of perfect blooms tucked into a folded napkin make all the difference. Sweetly-scented freesias are the perfect choice.

Daisy chain napkin ring for the children to make. Cut stems short. Make a slit in each and push the neighbouring stem through it. A charming idea which can also be used to decorate the base of a candle.

Pretty little eggshell vases are ideal Easter-time decorations — but why reserve them for Easter? This one holds a nosegay of primulas and the trailing foliage of 'mind your own business'.

MOTHER'S DAY TRIBUTE

There's no prettier way to say 'happy birthday', 'thank you for being such a nice Mum' or 'it's Valentine's Day and I've remembered!' than with a small floral posy on a breakfast tray. It's a charming notion, too, as a gesture to a weekend guest, a sick friend or relative, or for no special reason at all, but just on a sudden generous impulse.

If time is short, a single rose, particularly a finely scented bloom, in a display vase is hard to beat — but don't use a tall container that may be knocked over. Cylindrical glass tumblers, herb jars, stoneware mustard pots or cosmetic jars make simple stable containers. Egg cups make delightful flower holders; if scrambled eggs are on the menu, you can even use the broken eggshells, the jagged line around the top giving support to the flower stems. Don't fill the containers, however small, with water, especially if you have to negotiate a flight of stairs while carrying a loaded tray.

If you have time for a little secret planning in advance, you can create a tiny arrangement held in foam — in a delicate shell or sugar bowl. For a romantic occasion, an anniversary or Valentine's Day, a tiny posy of dried flowers is a specially lovely token that can be treasured.

Mother's Day tribute

This breakfast-tray nosegay (left) is full of love and gratitude. There's rosemary — that's for remembrance; pansies — they're for thoughts; lily-of-the-valley — they mean 'return of happiness'; blue grape hyacinths, for constancy, and forget-me-nots, so named as to speak for themselves. The lemon freesias and snow-white lilies are sweetly scented, and all-in-all the design is guaranteed to make any mother feel extra-special in every way.

The container is a tiny cream jug and the flower stems are held in a narrow block of foam extending 7.5 cm (3 in) above the rim. Broad-petalled pansies are skilled in the art of concealment!

Valentine heart posy

The heart-shaped posy is composed of a white anemone surrounded by fourteen deep red rose buds, gypsophila and frondy foliage. To achieve such a well-defined shape it is necessary to wire the flower stems so you can gently ease them this way and that. Instructions for wiring flowers and foliage are given on page 73.

To assemble the posy, hold the anemone in one hand and surround it with gypsophila. Arrange the red rose buds round it, coaxing them into the heart shape. Add more sprays of gypsophila and make a 'collar' of foliage enclosing the flowers.

Bind the stems firmly together with wire, then wrap them around with ribbon and finish with a bow.

Let your imagination have its way when you arrange the flowers for an informal buffet party. As long as they are totally in accord with the mood of the occasion, anything goes.

If the party is for a young age group, take a fresh look at containers. For a pasta or chilli party, you could group together a number of glass storage jars filled with pasta and pulses and use one of them to hold marigolds, ruby dahlias or fresh green herbs, or you might arrange flowers in a rice scoop or wooden storage jar. If you make a design in a dish or bowl, cover the holding foam with a handful of pasta shells or kidney beans. If several of the guests have a preference for health foods, arrange a basket of glowing vegetables — aubergines, peppers, tomatoes and so on — and tuck a few bay leaves and composite flowers, such as gaillardia or helenium, amongst them. Or pile up seasonal fruits garnished with just an occasional flower — *Alchemilla mollis* with apples and pears, mallow with black and green grapes, or any such combination that takes your fancy.

If all the guests belong to a particular club or work for the same political group, take the club or party colours as your springboard. Whatever the theme, you can aim to achieve even the most unseasonal of colour effects. Dye white flowers with coloured inks (see page 42) or cheat shamelessly and tuck a few paper or silk flowers amongst the foliage and fresh flowers.

A party-piece

The flowers on a buffet table should be as welcoming as the food itself, and will still draw admiring glances after the last dish is cleared. A tall container puts the flowers into better view and occupies little space on an already crowded table. Make sure the container is on a firm base — think of all those arms reaching across to the bread rolls — or weight it with sand or pebbles. Arrangements for a buffet party are generally more effective if they consist of a few well-defined flowers rather than a mass of tiny ones, which can fade into an obscure haze.

A collection of foliage in contrasting shades of blue- and yellow-greens can get your arrangement off to a good start — and will not be too demanding on the budget. You can highlight the greens with a few flowers in striking colours, as shown here, or use vivid fruits and cones, wired (see page 88) or speared on cocktail sticks.

A bowl of poppies

For a buffet party arrangement, go for simplicity with a dash of ostentation — a casual grouping of camellia and ivy leaves with a brilliant splash of single and double Icelandic poppies in all the sunshine colours.

Step 1 Fill the bowl with soaked foam to rise just above the rim. Cover it with crumpled wire, tied round the base of the container.
Step 2 Place the camellia and ivy leaves. Insert the flower buds that define the edges of the design.
Step 3 Arrange the poppies to give maximum impact, orange next to palest peach, deep scarlet alongside salmon pink. Insert more leaves to conceal the foam, if this is necessary.

Step 1   Step 2   Step 3

A BOWL OF POPPIES

A PILLAR OF FLOWERS

A pillar of flowers is often called for on very special family occasions to decorate a church or reception hall. The design opposite, shown on a painted wooden pedestal, would be equally suitable inside the church door, or repeated to form a matching pair on each side of the altar.

Before you set to work on a special pedestal arrangement, it might be helpful to read the general notes on page 18. These will guide you in the matter of planning, proportion and preparation.

Step 1 The container is a creamy pottery soup tureen raised on a shallow 'foot'. Place one whole block of soaked foam at the back, standing on end. Cut a second block in half and place one half in front of the full block. Cut the remaining piece in two again and place one foam strip at each side. Cover the foam with crumpled wire netting, tucking it inside the rim. Tie the netting securely with fine twine, securing it under the 'bowl' of the tureen.

Step 2 Place the lily stems in graduating heights with some of the flowers pointing downwards and extending below the rim of the container.

Step 3 Position the tall sprays of bronze single chrysanthemums towards the top and the golden lilies down the centre of the design, to be the focal point.

Step 4 Fill in with stocks, roses, anemones, freesias and narcissus. Add foliage to give weight at the base and at the rear of the design. Out of sight at the back, but providing a green background to the arrangement, there are large fatsia leaves. Lastly add sprays of gypsophila.

Keep the container topped up with water, spray the flowers with tepid water from an atomiser.

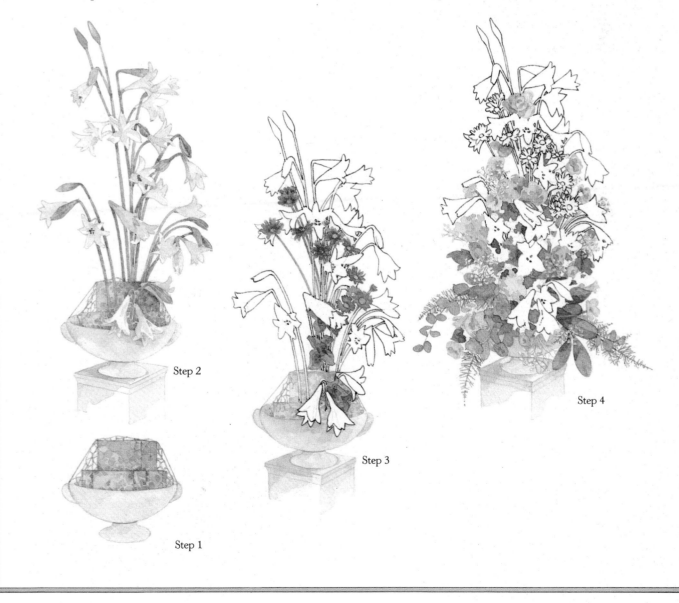

Step 2

Step 1

Step 3

Step 4

A wedding in the family offers a chance in a lifetime to celebrate with flowers, using a variety of lovely ideas — from a pedestal design in the church or hall to a romantic posy decorating the wedding cake. A floral swag outlining the table is a striking focal point and a beautiful frame for the happy bride and groom.

Flowers for a wedding need not be elaborate or too demanding in terms of time and money — often the simplest notions are the most effective. Humble shepherd's parsley creates a fine display in a pedestal arangement for a country wedding (right). The pretty scheme of spreading white flowers offset with heavier carnation blooms could also be used in arrangements for the reception room. For the centrepiece of a buffet table, fill a tall basket with frothy wild flowers, or use gypsophila as a garden alternative. For an autumnal wedding in a country church, with leaves turning gold on the trees all around, put in the rich colours of single chrysanthemums to catch the glowing mood.

Continuing the theme, use small blooms, buds and sprays of flowers to create miniature designs for each table at the reception. Small margarine or yogurt pots make perfectly good temporary containers and can be artfully concealed.

Flowers to decorate the cake can be arranged in a simple wine glass. Pink and white rosebuds, echoed in the cake's icing, are a traditional and very suitable choice — our arrangement includes freesias and a lacecap hydrangea, held in a champagne glass. It is an especially charming touch to plan the cake-top flowers as a permanent keepsake for the bride. Tiny rosebuds and daisies, a fragrant spray of freesias, a delicate posy of wired hyacinth and stephanotis blooms, could all be preserved in desiccants after the event, to stand as an everlasting memento.

On the day, stand the posy in a narrow-necked wine glass or small flower specimen vase secured, if need be, by a touch of glacé icing. Afterwards, preserve the whole posy as described on page 92. Unwrap any covering so stems, too, are fully dried. Sprinkle on drying powder very gently, so that it touches every petal surface. After a few days the decoration will emerge perfectly preserved.

Be lavish in a small way with flowers and leaves on the buffet table. A ring of scented pelargonium leaves is prettier than a doily as a base for cakes or sand-wiches; a spray of primulas or dried daisy flowers is more unusual than piped cream as decoration for a fruit mousse. A few flowerheads floating in small bowls along the length of a buffet table will stay fresh to the last serving. Turn to pages 44 and 45 for more ideas on the marriage of flowers and food.

A WEDDING TABLE SWAG

The champagne corks are popping, the celebrations under way, and all eyes are on the top table — and the floral decorations. A floral swag, or decorative garland, frames the table and draws attention to it without taking up any space.

You can make a swag of evergreens and flowers to outline any vertical feature — a doorway, arch or window, the front of a stage, an alcove, or pillar. According to the shape of the surface, a swag can be hung in loops, as on the wedding buffet table shown here or over a fireplace (see page 59), in an inverted L shape or as a narrow vertical strip. It can also be spiralled around a pillar as a church decoration for a wedding or festival.

The materials

For the foundation of the swag, you can use a length of rope about 6mm (¼ in) diameter, very thick, coarse string, strips of cloth torn from old sheets, or tights twisted and knotted together. Measure the table front, cut the string or rope with a little to spare, and pin it in place. Check that the loops fall in even curves. Trim the length accurately and measure and mark the centre of the rope.

Select a variety of evergreens in contrasting colours. Juniper, variegated ivy, privet and rosemary are interesting choices. For our swag (opposite), we used *Asparagus sparenduli* and cupressus. The light, lovely green 'ribbon' they produce is ideal for a summer wedding. The flowers should complement those used in other arrangements made for the occasion and often snippings and side shoots can be utilised to advantage. Pinks, composites such as single chrysanthemums, cornflowers and larkspur are among those that last well, but even wild flowers will usually stay fresh for a single showing, if they are left in water until the last possible moment. Fabric, good quality paper or even plastic flowers — there are particularly life-like Christmas roses — can be mixed with fresh ones. This is well worth considering in winter when fresh flowers are expensive and the choice limited. You could use a selection of the flowers used in the swag to decorate the top of the wedding cake.

A table swag

Step 1 Cut the evergreens into mixed bunches, two or three types together, in sprays about 12.5cm (5 in) long, and bind the stems with silver wire. (If you use *Asparagus sparenduli*, the bunches will be longer.) This is a job you can do several days in advance.

Step 2 Working from the ends towards the centre, wire the bunches of evergreen to the foundation, with the stem ends pointing towards the centre, and the top of each successive bunch covering the wired stems of the one before. Work one whole side first, then start from the centre again and work to the other end. Appraise the swag carefully and wire on extra evergreens to cover any gaps that may be apparent.

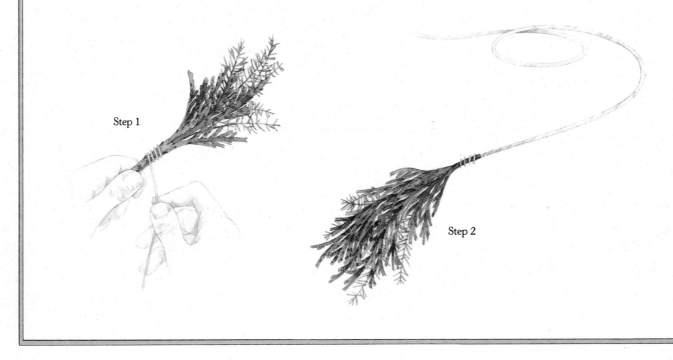

Step 1

Step 2

Step 3 Calculate roughly how many flowers you will need, whether you will have a spangled look from separate blooms at intervals, or an all-over floral effect — only practical really if you have access to a well-stocked garden. If you plan to use the flowers in tiny bunches — garden pinks and clippings of larkspur, or cornflowers and love-in-a-mist, for example — you can prepare them in advance. Cut the stems to about 4cm (1½ in) long, make up the little bunches and bind them with silver wire, leaving about 6cm (2½ in) ends of wire for tying the bunches to the swag.

Step 4 When you are ready to attach the flowers, divide them into two equal groups and work one side at a time. Tuck all the flower stems under the greenery, to conceal them, and bind them in place with the loose ends of wire.

Step 5 Attach the rope to the tablecloth using drawing pins, or sew it with a few stitches. Pay special attention to the points where the swag is attached and wire on extra flowers to neaten them. Tie large ribbon bows and wire them to the rope at these points as decorative finishing touches.

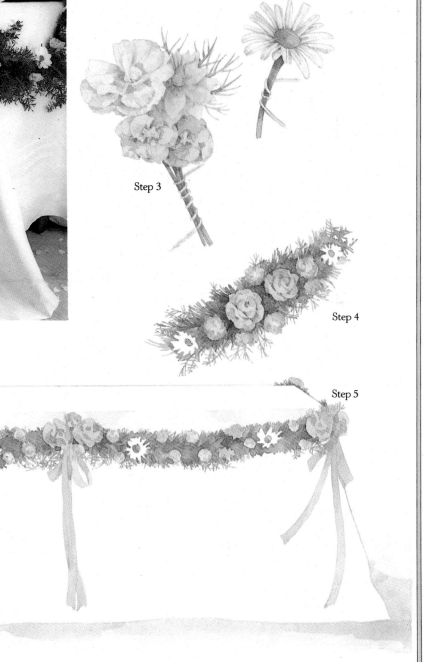

Step 3

Step 4

Step 5

paints are sold in a wide variety of colours including the metallic shades of gold, silver, bronze and copper. The metallic finishes are particularly effective while the vivid reds are cheerful and seasonal.

You can spray leaves all over with paint to disguise the natural colour completely, or just spatter them with 'raindrops' of colour, applying a couple of short sprays of paint from about 20cm (8 in) away. Select your plant materials and, before you start, cover the table and any nearby surfaces with newspaper.

If the birds have beaten you to the holly berries, here is a chance to triumph with your ingenuity. Use a bright red paint spray to intensify the colour of rose hips or to give a new look to clusters of blackish ivy berries. To spray a cluster of berries without colouring the leaves, cut a slit in a piece of card, slip it over the stem behind the berries and hold the nozzle close to them as you spray the paint.

To plan ahead for our window arrangement you need one can of silver and one of red paint. Lightly spray stems of spruce leaves and large pine cones with silver, to look as if they are just touched with frost. Spray mahonia leaves with solid colour and spatter others with silver moondrops — unusually attractive and more economical, too. Turn orange Chinese lanterns into silver bells by coating them completely.

Using red paint, spray rosehips to intensify their colour. Let them dry and spray a second coat. Shiny plant materials tend to reject the first application.

To make this design, choose a large jug or vase with a wide aperture to take the bulky stems, or use a deep casserole dish or pot. Crush a piece of wire netting and insert it in the container to extend about 5cm (2 in) above the rim.

Place the tall twigs first; these have been dried and cones attached to them. Add spruce leaves dappled with silver, followed by rosehips which have been sprayed red. Fill in the centre with holly (to which artificial berries have been wired), juniper and cupressus and arrange the spiky mahonia leaves, some of which have been sprayed completely with silver and others partially, at the sides. Add highlights, where needed, with honesty and Chinese lanterns sprayed silver, and wire silver-tinged cones to the twigs.

Arrange the scarlet gerberas in a group, making sure the stems reach into the water, and place the anemones in a cluster around the rim. As the flowers fade you can replace them with fresh blooms.

It's Christmas! With the sound of carols — and a touch of frost — in the air, the scene is set for a glittering floral display. There's no need to spend a fortune on flowers. Make a long-lasting arrangement of evergreens, brightened with dried and sprayed materials, and add the finishing touch of a few fresh flowers. Three vibrant red gerberas and a bunch of red anemones tinged with white add festive colour to a jug of twigs, cones and leaves. Red tulips or geraniums, or imitation poinsettias in silk or plastic would be handsome alternatives. Artificial blooms are helpful if you have no garden and flowers are scarce or shops closed over Christmas. Substitute dried or fabric flowers when the fresh ones have faded.

Spraying plant materials

Build up to your festive arrangement well in advance by spraying evergreen leaves, cones, twigs, seedheads and berries with paints from aerosol cans. Cans of craft

A WINTER SCENE STEALER

'The holly and the ivy', blended with other evergreen leaves, cones and dried or artificial flowers, make beautiful and traditional decorations for Christmas. The swag and Advent candle ring shown here take a little time to make, but both last well, without any water, throughout the festive season.

The evergreens

Variegated holly, its leaves tinged with pale cream, is more eye-catching than the plain, dark green varieties. Cupressus, with its matt, fern-like leaves, is a good contrast to glossy holly leaves, and there are varieties with leaf colours ranging from deepest green to icy blue-green and pale lime green. If these are hard to find, juniper leaves are a good alternative.

Look for long trails of ivy, useful for the vertical 'ropes' of a swag, stems of ivy complete with clusters of black berries, and a selection of large, plain or variegated leaves. Laurel, bay and magnolia are also good choices. Introduce touches of red with dyed artificial flowers (as shown here), silk or crepe papers flowers and clusters of plastic berries, especially if the holly has few berries or none at all. Large poinsettia bracts, glowing red candles and generous ribbon bows complete the scene.

A Christmas swag

Using thick cord or twine about 6mm (¼ in) in diameter, measure out a length to droop over the mantelpiece (but not too low or near the fire) and hang evenly at either side. Mark the centre.

Cut sprays of evergreens and bind them into small bunches, using lengths from a reel of fine silver wire to secure them. Working from the centre, first to one end of the cord and then the other, and keeping the design symmetrical, attach the wired greenery. (See page 54 for detailed instructions.)

Fix the small red flowers at various points along the length of the swag. Wire the cones (see page 88) and bind them in place. Hang the swag over the mantelpiece, using drawing pins, tacks or adhesive clay to secure it. Tie in the poinsettias at each corner. Check the overall effect of the swag carefully and wire on more leaves to fill in any gaps. Tie the bows and wire them in place.

The Advent ring

You can make an Advent ring to form a table centrepiece which is firmly based in a foam ring. You can buy such a ring, but it is easy to make one yourself by placing 5cm (2 in) high blocks of foam around the inside of an upturned biscuit tin lid (fig 1).

First position the four candles, using holders to secure them, then decorate the foam base around them with sprays of holly. Fill in the gaps with wired cones, red artificial flowers and sprays of white statice. Fix a large red bow at two sides (fig 2).

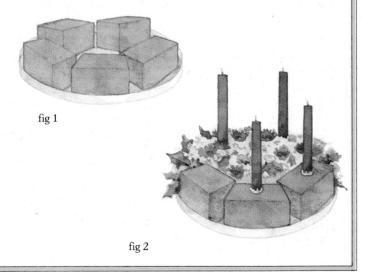

fig 1

fig 2

A CHRISTMAS SWAG

Celebrate the first festival of springtime, when we rejoice in the blossoming of so many bright and beautiful flowers, with a floral basket filled to overflowing.

You can buy tiny handled baskets, about 6cm (2½ in) across, in charity shops and these make cheap and cheerful flower containers. Line them with foil, insert a piece of soaked foam and arrange a few colourful primulas, dainty primroses or anemones. Just one of these little flower baskets is enough to brighten an early-morning tray or decorate an Easter cake. For a table centre with a difference, stand a catkin twig in a narrow container or a pinholder and hang several floral baskets and coloured egg shells from its slender branches.

Brighten a fireplace with the colours of spring by standing an inner container in a garden basket and filling it with a mass of flowers — the impact of a single colour, such as bright yellow daffodils, can be casually stunning.

Take a breath of spring with you when you visit friends and relations. A gypsy basket of violets, each little bunch ringed round with leaves and primroses, is a delightful gift.

Posy time

Primroses and violets seem made for each other, whether they are arranged into a delightful posy to be carried, and later to stand in a container, or clustered in tiny bunches the way children like to group them. Our basket of posies, reminiscent of traditional gypsy flower baskets, holds a mass of delicate flowers gathered from a spring garden.

Step 1 Hold a rose in one hand, surround it with a circle of primroses, then with bunches of violets, about twelve at a time.

Step 2 For the outer ring, alternate grape hyacinths and small, pastel-coloured roses. Encircle the posy with primrose leaves. Adjust the arrangement so that the flowers are evenly spaced. Bind the stems with wire, trim them neatly and cover them with ribbon.

An Easter basket

Step 1 To form the primrose posies, make a 'pad' of four or five primrose leaves and secure the stems with a small elastic band. Bunch together about twelve primroses and bind them to the leaves or secure with an elastic band.

Step 2 To make the violet posies, bunch together about twenty-five violets and ring them with four deep green ivy leaves. Bind the stems or secure them with an elastic band.

Line a basket with an inner container, cover the top with flat wire netting and fill with water. Arrange the posies at random, or, as shown here, with the primroses tracing a flowing S shape.

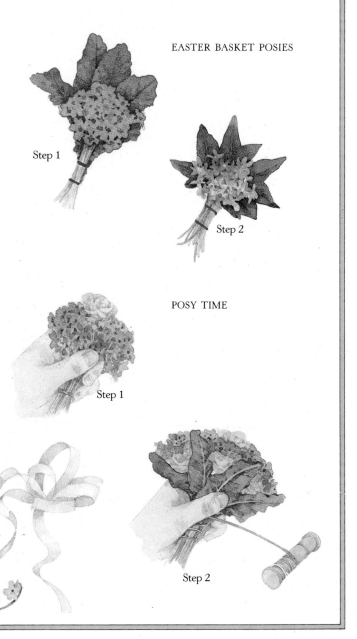

EASTER BASKET POSIES

Step 1

Step 2

POSY TIME

Step 1

Step 2

AN EASTER BASKET

FLOWERS TO CARRY & WEAR

A bouquet carried by a bride or presented to a visiting speaker; a fresh posy for a hat or headdress; a gift for a sick friend, party hostess or someone who has just moved house — flowers that must go where you go, whether on a short journey or as a day-long decoration, need special attention in arrangement and conditioning.

Flowers that are worn or carried may have to be wired, to keep them in place and make handling easier. When you make an arrangement as a gift, why not choose a particularly pretty or unusual container, as part of your offering. Sweet-smelling herbs or lavender can be bound in a garland, for gifts that are both practical and ornamental.

You can make sure a special message goes with your gift by rediscovering the language of flowers, a popular notion in Victorian times. Find in these pages the specific meanings that can be conveyed by a single bloom or a combination of flowers designed with care.

The symbolic meaning of flowers is beautifully ex-
pressed by Shakespeare's Ophelia, who tells us,
> 'There's rosemary — that's for remembrance;
> Pray love remember; and there is pansies —
> That's for thoughts.'

Throughout the ages flowers have been presented and
carried as symbols of love, affection, gratitude, sympathy, respect — or just 'for thoughts'. The intriguing
language of flowers is more fully described on page 66.

There can be no prettier way of conveying any
message than assembling a nosegay of flowers. To
achieve a florist's professionalism does, it is true, take
considerable training. To achieve a pleasing arrangement is within the scope of each of us — and after all,
it's the thought that counts.

When you are arranging flowers to be carried, there
are a few special points to consider. In the case of a gift
arrangement this may be little more than the careful
choice of a suitable container. Where bridal and other
formal flower designs are concerned, it can be
an advantage to master a few elementary wiring
techniques.

Make your selection of flowers and foliage from
those that have specially long-lasting qualities or are
known for their resilience — single chrysanthemums,
lilies, carnations, cornflowers, pinks, zinnias, polyanthus, roses and many other flowers; also ivy, clematis,
bay and ferns. You will find helpful notes in the A to Z
(beginning on page 107). And of course, all flowers and
leaves for presentation, which may be out of water for
some time, must be conditioned with extra care (see
pages 12 and 13).

Flowers as gifts

Flowers make a perfect gift for any occasion. Your gift
will be doubly welcome if the flowers are already
arranged, or presented as a sheaf or posy that can be
put straight into water. A flurried hostess with count-
less last-minute jobs to do will bless you for your
thoughtfulness! Another idea, especially appreciated by
friends without a garden and by the partially sighted, is
a scented lavender ring (see page 74).

When you offer a ready-made arrangement, the
container can represent part of your gift — a pretty
basket, wooden trug, special cup and saucer, or fluted
flan dish would all be suitable. Where the container is
concealed by the flowers and does not form part of the
arrangement, you can choose from such inexpensive
items as a shallow plastic bulb bowl, a florist's plastic
saucer-shaped holder on a short stand, a used preserve
jar, or even a margarine tub.

The choice of holding material and mechanics will
be influenced to an extent by the size and shape of the
container but soaked plastic foam is usually preferable.
This is because it both provides a constant moisture
source and holds stems rigidly in place.

Leaves — the natural protectors

Design your arrangement so that the flowers are
protected by leaves at every likely contact point — at
the base of the design (where they will also add visual
weight), at the top and sides.

Keep the design simple and avoid using tall stems
which might snap. The most suitable styles to choose
are compact triangles or circular, domed cushion
shapes, designed in a round container.

Many of these principles apply when you are
arranging presentation sprays, posies or bouquets to be
carried. It is no coincidence that traditional Victorian
posies, circlets of single flowers around a central
rosebud, were ringed by ivy or fern leaves and sometimes also a collar of lace, to protect the flowers.

Flowers that are to be carried should be comfortable
to hold. A sheaf of flowers must rest easily across the
arm and not be top-heavy.

More stylized posies and bouquets are made possible
if the flowers and leaves are first wired, so that they can
be more readily coaxed into place (see page 73). Wiring
also extends the range of flowers you can use —
individual polyanthus flowers, tiny spray pinks,
hyacinth bells, and apple blossom, for example.

Heady ideas

Fresh flowers make delightful hair decorations, in the
form of a headband or circlet, and a small posy or
garland of flowers can make a plain hat more elegant.

For a wedding headdress, select flowers that perfectly match or complement those being carried, and take
hair colour into account, contrasting blooms of a light
or dark tone against very dark or fair hair.

While you're in the mood, and have a few snippets
of flowers and foliage left over, why not form them into
miniature sprays or posies to decorate a gift parcel?

There's quite an art in composing a spray of flowers to present to a visiting VIP. This selection of enchanting pale lemon day lilies, delicate pink roses, spray carnations and deep mauve anemones is composed very simply, layer upon layer and without wiring. Busy ladies will bless you for your thoughtfulness — it is all ready to lower gently into a tall, deep container without further arranging.

For the backing, choose evergreen foliage that will last well indoors. Avoid very dark-coloured leaves or those with a dense, matt surface. They can make the spray seem heavy and dull. The choice here is eucalyptus; the soft grey-green leaves perfectly complement the pastel-coloured flowers. Camellia, golden privet and spotted laurel leaves would be equally suitable. Be sure to select a few flowers with very long stems to give height to the design, as the lilies do here. Spray chrysanthemums, mallow, salvia, verbascum or primula japonica would be pretty alternatives.

The spray

Step 1 Decide on the length of your spray — this is 45cm (18 in) long — and cut the foliage accordingly. Place a few of the longest sprays of leaves on the table and cut others slightly shorter to place at the sides. Arrange the tallest lilies in the centre.

Step 2 Place the flowers in order of height, alternating the colours — the lemon with the pink. Arrange the roses, one at the base and two at the centre, and place the anemones to accent the sides with dark colour.

Step 3 Cut short sprays of carnations and place them in a cluster beneath the other flowers. Carefully pick up the spray and arrange a few flowers behind the foliage, so that the back view is also decorative. Bind the stems tightly with twine or wire. Tuck in the wire ends securely amongst the stems to protect small hands. Finish with a ribbon bow.

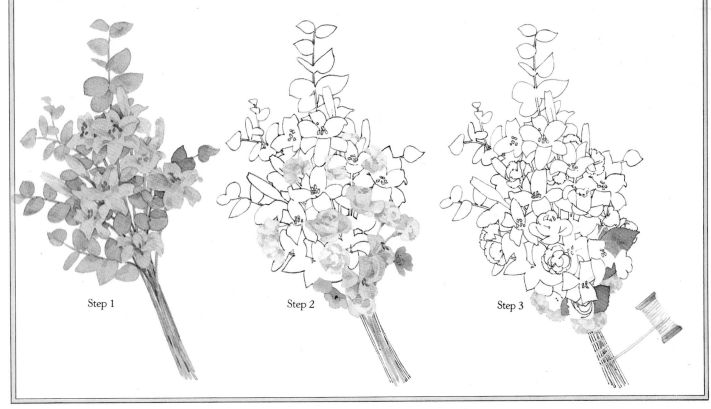

Step 1   Step 2   Step 3

The gentle art of saying it with flowers, of expressing tender thoughts without a word being spoken or written, has its roots in age-old customs. For centuries lovers have known that a single blossom or a simple posy can speak volumes and indeed often had a very literal and universally understood meaning. A sprig of yellow mimosa, passed surreptitiously to a girl, would tell, for example, of a young man's secret love, while a calceolaria flower offered even better prospects in saying 'I offer you my fortune'. In reply, a woman could toss into her suitor's path a striped carnation, meaning refusal, a white carnation denoting her coyness or a yellow one her disdain.

Touch a flower you are given to your lips and in the language of flowers it means 'yes'. Pull off a petal and let it fall to the ground and you have indicated 'no'. In Victorian times, when the symbolic and poetic language of flowers was a familiar form of communication, whole sentences could be conveyed in two or three flowers. When words almost fail to express the depth of one's concern, thrift flowers and red poppies suffice: 'Please accept my sympathy. May you find consolation.' A posy of white bellflower, signifying gratitude, is a pretty way of saying thank you; a sprig of sweet basil is a delightful way to convey good wishes, and a bunch of ox-eye daisies a beautiful token of love.

All this may seem an anachronism in today's world but there are times when the sentimental language of the past can add charm to an occasion. If you are arranging flowers for a wedding, anniversary or Valentine party, sending a basket of wild or garden blooms to someone who is sick or alone, or want to express feelings you can scarcely put into words, look through this list of meanings, and say it with flowers.

Almond, flowering, hope

Aloe, grief, bitterness

Alyssum, sweet, worth beyond beauty

Amaryllis, pride, haughtiness

Anemone, forsaken

Apple blossom, preference

Aster, China
   double, 'I echo your sentiments'
   single, 'I will think of it'

Azalea, temperance

Balsam, red, 'don't touch me'

Balsam, white, 'Busy Lizzie', impatience

Basil, hatred

Belladonna lily, silence, a falsehood

Bellflower, white, gratitude

Betony, surprise

Bluebell, constancy

Broom, neatness, humility

Bryony, prosperity

Bugloss, a falsehood

Buttercup, childishness

Calceolaria, 'I offer you my fortune'

Californian poppy, 'do not refuse me'

Camellia
   red, unpretentiousness
   white, perfect loveliness

Campanula, blue, gratitude

Candytuft, indifference

Carnation,
   pink, a woman's love
   red, 'my heart is breaking'
   striped, refusal
   white, coyness
   yellow, disdain

Cherry blossom,
   pink, insincerity
   white, deception

China rose, renewed beauty

Christmas rose, 'put me out of my misery!'

Chrysanthemum,
   red, 'I love'
   white, truth
   yellow, slighted love

Cineraria, always agreeable

Clarkia, 'I love your conversation'

Clematis, a beautiful mind

Coltsfoot, 'justice shall be done'

Coreopsis, always cheerful

Cowslip, winning grace

Crocus, cheerfulness

Crown imperial, majesty, power

Currant, 'I'll die if you frown'

Daffodil, regard

Dahlia,
   red, instability
   white, single mindedness
   yellow, caution

Daisy,
   garden, 'I share your sentiments'
   wild, 'I will think of it'

Daphne, glory, immortality

Day lily, coquetry

Dog rose, pleasure mixed with pain

Elderflower, compassion

Everlasting pea, everlasting pleasure

Fern, sincerity

Forget-me-not, remembrance

Foxglove, insincerity, a wish

French marigold, jealousy

Fuchsia, taste, gracefulness

Gardenia, refinement

Geranium,
   lemon-scented, unexpected
      meeting
   oak-leaved, true friendship
   pink, preference
   red, comforting
   wild, steadfast piety

Gladioli, armed

Gorse, all-year-round love

Hawthorn, hope

Hazel, reconciliation

Heather, solitude

Heliotrope, faithfulness

Hibiscus, delicate beauty

Holly, 'have you forgotten me?'

Hollyhock, ambition

Honesty, sincerity

Honeysuckle,
   cultivated, 'I will take my
      time to answer'

Hyacinth,
   blue, constancy
   purple, sorrow
   red, playfulness
   white, loveliness

Hydrangea, heartlessness

Iris,
   blue, 'my compliments'
   yellow, passion

Ivy, friendship, marriage

Jasmine, amiability

Jonquil, 'I want you to return
   my love'

Laburnum, pensive beauty

Lady's slipper, fickleness

Larkspur, lightness
   pink, fickleness
   double, haughtiness

Laurel leaves, glory

Lavender, distrust

Lilac,
   purple, beginnings of love
   white, purity, modesty

Lily,
   white, purity
   yellow, gaiety

Lily of the valley, return of
   happiness

Lobelia, malevolence

London pride, frivolity

Love-in-a-mist, perplexity

Love-lies-bleeding, undying love

Magnolia, love of nature

Marigold, uneasiness

Michaelmas daisy, cheerfulness
   in old age

Mimosa, secret love

Mint, virtue

Mistletoe, 'I overcome all
   obstacles'

Mountain ash, 'you are safe
   with me'

Myrtle, love

Narcissus, self-esteem

Nasturtium, patriotism

Oak leaves, bravery, courage

Oleander, 'beware!'

Olive branch, peace

Orange blossom, purity

Pansy. 'I think of you, think of
   me'

Passion flower, belief, suscepti-
   bility

Pear blossom, affection

Peony, bashfulness

Periwinkle, pleasant memories

Petunia, 'I find your presence
   soothing'

Pink, 'hurry up!', boldness
   clover, enduring sweetness
   red double, pure, undying
      love
   variegated, refusal
   white, talent

Polyanthus, pride of riches

Poppy,
   red, consolation
   white, sleep

Ranunculus, 'you are very
   attractive'

Rhododendron, danger at hand

Rock rose, popular favour

Rosa mundi, merriment

Rose, love
   bud, red, young girl
   bud, white, a heart without
      love
   bud, moss, hidden love
   cabbage, messenger of love
   moss, superiority
   musk, capricious beauty
   red, beauty, 'I love you'
   single, simplicity
   white, 'I am worthy of you'
   wild, simplicity
   yellow, infidelity

Rosebay, 'beware'

Rose leaf, 'you may hope'

Rosemary, remembrance

Rudbekia, justice

Rue, disdain

Sage, esteem

Salvia, red, energy

Shamrock, lightheartedness

Snapdragon, 'no'

Snowdrop, consolation, hope

Stephanotis, 'will you come with
   me?'

Stock, lasting beauty

Sunflower, haughtiness

Sweet basil, best wishes

Sweet briar, poetry

Sweet pea, delicate pleasures

Sweet William, gallantry

Syringa, memory

Tendrils, of any plant, bands,
   ties

Thrift, sympathy

Thyme, activity, courage

Tulip, fame
   red, declaration of love
   variegated, beautiful eyes
   yellow, hopeless love

Verbena,
   pink, family unity
   red, unity
   white, 'pray for me'

Veronica, fidelity

Violet,
   blue, faithfulness, candour
   purple, 'I think of you'
   white, innocence, modesty
   wild, idle love

Wallflower, fidelity even in mis-
   fortune

Water lily, falsehood, gaiety

Wisteria, welcome, stranger

Yew, sorrow

Xeranthemum, cheerfulness in
   adversity

Zinnia, thinking of absent
   friends

A BRIDAL BOUQUET AND POSY

Charmingly informal for a summer wedding and romantically pretty in pink and white flowers, this bridal bouquet and matching bridesmaid's posy are simple to make.

If you are making them for a friend's wedding, ask the bride for a small sample of the dress fabrics, or arrange to peep at the dresses, so that you can match the colours exactly or choose clear contrasts. For complete co-ordination of both colours and styles, find out also what kind of flower arrangements will be used to decorate the church.

Choice of materials

For a long spray design, slender trails of leaves make a pretty contrast between the delicate fabric of the wedding dress and the fresh blooms of the flowers. Variegated ivy edged with cream, ferns, clematis, eucalyptus, rosemary and periwinkle are all good choices. Short sprays of silver-leaved plants such as *Senecio*, provide a pretty and informal background to the bridesmaid's posy.

In your selection of flowers, include flat shapes, sprays, trumpets and buds, which are particularly useful for the tip of a tapering design, and plan the colours carefully. In our bridal bouquet the pink and white colouring of the *Hemerocallis* lilies picks up both the pink of the carnations and the white of the single chrysanthemums, freesias, lily-of-the-valley and gypsophila. In the smaller posy, bright pink nerines are substituted for the lilies.

Condition both foliage and flowers (see page 12) before beginning the designs. Once the flowers are assembled, spray them with cool water and keep them in a cool room away from the light.

The bridal bouquet

The bouquet shown here is an example of an unwired spray, equally suitable when carried by a bride or presented to a special guest on another occasion — for an anniversary or speech day, perhaps.

Arrange the longest foliage, buds and flowers flat on a table and check the length and width. Cut flower stems in graduating lengths and build them up on top of the first layer (see page 65), placing one perfect bloom (a lily) in the centre for the focal point, and a cluster of flowers (the single chrysanthemums) close to the hand-grip. Check that the sides of the design are tapered and symmetrical.

Bind the stems with fine silver wire, and then with florist's tape. Bend the wired stems slightly to form a handle. Finish with a bow and trailing ribbons.

The bridesmaid's posy

To make the bridesmaid's informal posy, cut the flower stems to almost equal lengths, with longer sprays of evergreen foliage (rosemary — that's for remembrance!) and short sprays of silver leaves (*Senecio*).

Step 1 Group together the three or four flowers that will form the centre and bind the stems with wire. Add more flowers all the way round, arranging each one separately and at a slight angle, and wire the stems in place.

Step 2 Continue to add flowers and foliage, turning the posy slightly as each piece is bound in. Wind florist's tape around the stems, bend them slightly to form a handle and finish with a ribbon bow.

Step 1

Step 2

Bride, bridesmaid, wedding guest, garden party enthusiast — on special occasions flowers can literally go to your head. Make a flowered headdress or decorate a summery straw hat to grace a memorable moment.

Headdresses

Small pink roses are entwined in miniature bunches with dainty variegated ivy, gypsophila and pink blossom to make these enchanting headdresses. The method is similar in each case — the headband is composed of six roses and the circlet of ten.

Step 1 Cut the stem of each rose to about 1.5cm (½ in) long and push in a 6cm (2½ in) length of florist's wire. Bind the wire with green florist's tape. Arrange the roses, ivy and gypsophila into tiny posies and bind the stems of each with florist's wire.

Step 2 Measure a piece of florist's wire the required length for circlet or headband and bind it with green florist's tape. Working from the centre outwards and using wire from a roll, bind the rose posies to the holding wire with the flowers facing away from the centre. Arrange each rose to conceal the stems of the neighbouring posy. Wire a slender sprig of blossom to extend beyond the last rose. Repeat from the centre along the other side. Tie a narrow ribbon with long trails close to each end of the headband. A large bow with trailing ends finishes the centre back of the circlet.

Step 1

Step 2

Flowery hats

A plain straw boater takes on a positively frivolous air when it is encircled with pastel-coloured flowers. Our choice is cream fuchsias and a pale lemon hyacinth paired with tiny sprigs of white gypsophila and small-leaved evergreen foliage. Check the number of flowers and leaf sprays you need by placing them loosely around the brim of the hat, the hyacinth at the back and the fine foliage tips just meeting at the front.

Step 1 Cut hyacinth flowers 7.5cm (3 in) from the tip and push a wire through the stem, leaving about 5cm (2 in) of bare wire. Bind this with green florist's tape. Make tiny bunches of freesia flowers and bind with the gypsophila and foliage. Secure the stems with roll wire.

Step 2 Bind the flower posies first to the hyacinth stem and then to each other until the strip goes half-way around the brim, then repeat the sprays, working from the hyacinth around the other side. Place the circlet of flowers around the hat brim. Secure it with a stitch in two places.

For the child's hat, make two rose posies as described for the headdresses. Bind the stems together with the roses facing away from each other. Bind a third rose between them, covering the stems. Secure the flowers to the hat with a couple of stitches.

Step 1

Step 2

FLOWER-DECKED HATS

VICTORIAN-STYLE BRIDAL BOUQUET

For such a special day the bride should carry flowers that particularly complement her clothes. Make a dainty, Victorian-style bridal bouquet that has a natural fresh appeal and charm of its own.

The bouquet is created from sunshine-yellow and white roses, alstroemeria and freesia, tapering foliage fronds and small-leaved evergreens. Each flower is wired to a false stem and the stems bound with all-concealing green florist's tape. Wiring admittedly takes a little time and practice but the effort is rewarded — wired flowers can be positioned accurately and are more easily carried. A posy of unwired flower stems, especially if it includes woody ones such as roses and camellias, can be bulky to handle.

To make the bouquet, follow the instructions on this page to wire the flowers and foliage. Bind all the wire stems with green gutta percha. Cut short lengths of fine evergreen leaves.

To assemble the bouquet, start with the yellow rose in the centre and surround it with white freesias, then with alstroemeria alternating with yellow rosebuds. Encircle the posy with sprigs of foliage and evergreen leaves. Adjust the shape and bind the stems with wire and ribbon.

Spray the flowers with tepid water and place them in a cool, dark place until they are needed, away from sunlight or any source of heat.

The illustrations below show various ways to wire flowers suitable for a bouquet. Practise these methods before the occasion.

Wiring flowers for bouquets and posies

Flowers with brittle, fine, fleshy or damaged stems, and flowers to be used together in a large bouquet (when removing the stem lessens their weight), benefit from being cut very short and wired externally. Push a wire through the base of the flower head (fig 1), pull it through and bend the ends down parallel with the stem. Twist them to criss-cross around the stem (fig 2).

Flower heads with no stem can be cross-wired (useful for preventing buds opening). Push two light wires at right angles through the base (fig 3) bend them down and twist them to form a false stem (fig 4).

Lilies, alstroemeria and orchids can be wired by the 'hairpin' method. Bend a florist's wire into a hairpin-shaped hook about 2.5cm (1 in) long but with one end longer than the other. Place it over the stem (fig 5) and twist the long end around both the stem and the short end (fig 6).

To wire roses, cut the stems to about 4cm (1½ in) long. Push a florist's wire through the stem and into the flower. Bind the rose calyx and the wire with green gutta percha (fig 7).

To wire foliage, place a florist's wire along the stem and bind the two together with gutta percha (fig 8).

fig 1   fig 2   fig 3   fig 4

fig 5   fig 6   fig 7   fig 8

Step 1

Convey your message, whether it is one of congratulation, joy, sympathy or a simple 'thank you', with a gift of flowers. Choose a basket of mixed flowers or a delightfully old-fashioned scented lavender ring, like the one shown on this page, and your sincerity — and talent — will be in no doubt.

Lavender ring

A delightful alternative to a lavender bag — and you don't even have to thread a needle! The ring makes a pretty ornament for the bedroom wall, or it can be hung inside a wardrobe or placed in a drawer to give your special clothing a delicate fragrance.

Make a circle from a 35cm (14 in) length of stout wire (which can be cut from a wire coathanger) and bind the join. Hang it on a piece of ribbon and work from the centre top first to one side and then the other. Using fine silver wire, bind on small bunches of lavender, the heads facing away from the centre on either side. Make a large bunch of lavender, or wheat heads if available, and wire them to hang into the circle. Bind the stems with ribbon and finish with a ribbon bow for a really decorative effect.

Step 2

Step 3

Fruit and flowers make an admirable gift when you are going to stay with friends or want to give something personal with just a hint of flattery. Who would not be pleased to receive a basket generously filled to overflowing with a pineapple, bunches of luscious grapes and a sun-burst of garden or market flowers?

The pineapple gives a colour cue; the lovely soft apricot tone is picked up in sprays of lilies and single chrysanthemums; a touch of white added with pheasant's eye narcissus and daisy-like chrysanthemums. The softly curving stems of hellebores repeat the pale green of the pineapple frond and the shiny black-skinned grapes provide a tempting contrast.

The gift basket

Fill the basket with damp, downy moss to make a natural-looking 'cushion' for the fruit and flowers. You can buy moss at many florists' shops, or substitute straw or crumpled crepe or tissue paper. A mossy base contributes more to the overall effect, but paper can be artfully concealed by careful placing of the flowers.

Step 1 Place a block of soaked foam on the moss. If using a paper base, wrap the lower part of the foam in foil. Position the pineapple. Twist fine roll wire round the frond and secure it to the edge of the basket. Wire some grapes to the pineapple top to secure them.
Step 2 Strip the leaves from the lily stems. Position the tallest lilies in a diagonal line beside the pineapple. Cover the foam with hellebores, letting them spill over the basket rim. Push single lily flowers between them.
Step 3 Fill the design with single chrysanthemums and narcissus. Arrange large ivy leaves around the pineapple and deep green hellebore leaves on the opposite side. Wire a small bunch of grapes to the right hand side of the basket. Tie a ribbon bow to the handle and wire on a few flowers for effect.

FLOWERS FOR DISPLAY

Whatever the time and trouble you take over your flower arrangements at home, there is bound to be more planning involved in creating a special display for a particular location and occasion, when your flowers are on public view. If you are active on behalf of your local church or school, or are a member of a guild, club or society, there will be important dates in the calendar when a flamboyant display of flowers will be needed. In the following pages you will find sound advice on both designing your floral display and planning the sequence of work, on the day itself and in preparation for it, to ensure that you can avoid any last-minute panic.

Floral decorations for a church give year-round opportunities to try out different plant materials and styles of arrangement. Fit the flowers to the architectural features, as in our windowsill design of fresh spring flowers, or reflect the atmosphere of a special celebration, as in the central showpiece of the harvest festival display.

So often a ring round an important date on your calendar is also a reminder, that some extra-special flower arrangements are called for, to set the scene. Perhaps a popular personality is coming to open a local fête, give the school prizes or address a gathering in the public hall. Perhaps it is your turn on the rota to decorate the church, or you have been asked to contribute a design for a flower festival. In any event, the challenge is an exciting one which need not be in the least daunting.

Plan your showpiece step by step; you will find that you can use many of the same techniques that you apply when you arrange flowers for your home.

Make a site inspection

First of all, check the location. Make an appointment to go to the church or hall to see exactly where flowers are needed, or allowed. Some vicars do not permit flowers on the altar or the font, and at certain times in the church calendar there will be other restrictions, so check first. Make a note of all the appropriate measurements, that is the height and width of an alcove, the distance between the curtain and the front of the stage, the width of a windowsill and height of a window, the dimensions of a pew-end if you are creating a floral aisle for a bride. Then make rough sketches of the area concerned. (Just a reminder of the angle of a niche or the shape of a pillar can be helpful later.)

Study the situation from all angles. Check how light or dark it is and note the colour and texture of the background. Stand as far away from the spot as you can and note that some members of the congregation or audience must be able to admire your design from that distance.

Check what containers, if any, are available on the spot. Many churches have pedestals and large vases that have served generations of flower arrangers. If you are asked to decorate the church for a wedding or christening, find out who has responsibility for the flowers on that date, and ask permission to take over.

Plan of action

Decide what containers you need and beg, borrow or improvise them. If you cannot hire a pedestal, for example, you might be able to create a similar effect by placing an arrangement of generous proportions on a slender wine table or small cupboard. If you need a particularly large or specially narrow container — many a garden bucket or old baking tin has been well-disguised under a coat of washable emulsion paint!

Choose your colour scheme carefully, bearing in mind that the flowers must be seen at their best, even on a dull day or against a 'busy' background. It might also be worth finding out what flowers, in the case of a wedding, the bride is carrying and emphasising those colours. Make a sketch, however rough, of your designs, checking the proportions against your original notes. By drawing the shape and filling it in with coloured felt-tip pens, you can get a realistic idea of the effect.

Take early soundings among your friends to see who can promise you a supply of flowers. Make a list of what you need and what's on offer and calculate the likely cost. If you are arranging flowers for a club or public meeting and the committee has agreed to meet the expense, get your estimate approved in advance.

Gather together all the bits and pieces you will need, the secateurs, floral scissors, wire cutters, roll and stub wires, a watering can with a long spout to top up containers and a fine-mist spray to refresh the flowers. Don't forget large polythene sheets and newspapers to cover the floor where you will be working.

Allow yourself plenty of time to condition the foliage and flowers, bearing in mind that they might be on show for several days.

On the day

With your design meticulously planned and so much of the preparatory work behind you, carrying out the arrangements should be pure pleasure.

Give yourself plenty of space in which to work. Divide your plant materials into sections — foliage, focal points, fillers and so on. If you are creating two or more arrangements which must match, divide the materials between them accordingly. Stand back from the arrangement time and again, viewing it from the front and from each side, to check that it looks balanced and pleasing from every angle. Perhaps the most important point of all is to be sure you know when to stop. Too many flowers can look muddled from a distance.

Before you leave, top up the containers with water and, especially in hot weather, lightly spray the flowers.

A prize display

The whole community is in festive mood, there are prizes to be presented, and congratulations are the order of the day. Here we show you how to make sure that your flower display wins a few compliments!

Our collection of late spring flowers includes tulips and hyacinths, both of which benefit from having a florist's wire pushed up through the centre of the stem to stop them drooping.

Fill the bowl with a thick block of foam, cover it with crumpled wire netting and tie it under the bowl with fine white twine. Punch a hole in the foam with a skewer before inserting each flower.

Step 1 Position long sprays of eucalyptus or similar foliage, one at the centre and one trailing low on each side. Place shorter sprays at intervals across the design. Insert the white tulips to follow the triangular shape.
Step 2 Cover the stems of the tall central tulips with two cream hyacinths in graded heights and arrange cream hyacinths at the sides. Position the deep blue hyacinths and then the dark anemones, some pressed close against the foam. Follow these with the pale peach-coloured roses.
Step 3 Fill in with yellow and white ranunculus, and with yellow tulips projecting well beyond the level of the other flowers, to avoid a two-dimensional effect. Lastly, fill in with foliage.

Don't forget all flower arrangements must be neat and tidy and properly 'weighted' at the back. Often the guest of honour sees only the back view.

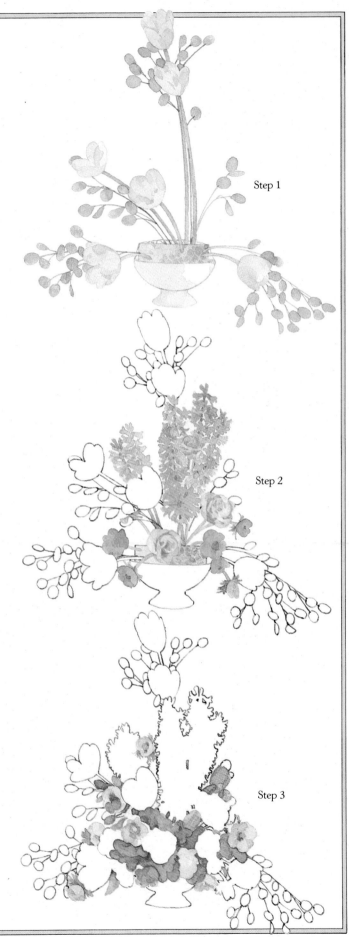

Step 1

Step 2

Step 3

A CHURCH WINDOW DESIGN

Arranging flowers for a church is always a very special task. Your designs will be displayed in what may be a beautiful and somewhat awe-inspiring setting, and will certainly add considerably to the joy and significance of the occasion. There are hints on page 78 to help you with the planning and preparation so that you can tackle small or large displays with equal confidence.

Several designs throughout the book are especially suited to display in a church — the pedestal arrangement on page 50 could be carried out on each side of the altar screen, the formal arrangement on page 76 would be appropriate to stand on a table or chest. The pillar of flowers, (see page 52), would add a lighter touch to the festivities. Portions of the wedding-day swag (see page 53) can be devised for decoration of pillars or pew-ends, and if flowers are permitted on the altar, the delightful seasonal designs in the First Things First chapter at the beginning of the book will give you all-year-round inspiration.

The design for a windowsill, opposite, is an example of one created in a 'hidden' container, a 1 kg (2 lb) loaf tin painted with cream emulsion paint. The young, fresh greens of the foliage make a delicate foil for the soft pastel colours of the spring flowers and help to conceal the container.

The window design

A classic L-shape is the perfect design to fit within the lines of a narrow window. The outline is emphasised by the long, slender stems of fern which are covered and partially veiled by thin trails of pink and red broom.

The container, deliberately concealed, is a large baking dish painted to merge with the stone. A block of foam extending 5cm (2 in) above the rim is held in place by criss-crossing elastic bands.

Step 1 Draw in the L-shape with long stems of fern and cover them with sprays of broom. Place the *Schefflera* leaves at the base and on the left. Strip the leaves and position the mauve and white freesias.
Step 2 Push a wire through the stem of each cream hyacinth to keep it upright, and put them in place. Position the pink tulips and add the tall rose.
Step 3 Fill in with pink spray carnations. Strip leaves from the deep pink fuchsias before inserting the stems and add the central rose as a focal point. Complete the design with short sprays of foliage.

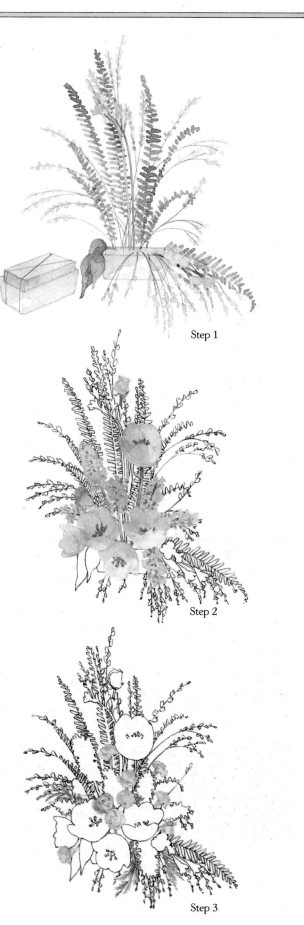

Step 1

Step 2

Step 3

MELLOW FRUITFULNESS

As the season of mellow fruitfulness comes round, churches are decorated in thanksgiving for a bountiful harvest, and it seems fitting that our gardens will also yield the glorious flowers and fruits of late summer. Dahlias, chrysanthemums and zinnias in all their vibrant colours, sprays of Michaelmas daisies in soft tones, boughs of ruby-red berries, hips and haw, branches of leaves beginning to change into their autumnal tints, baskets of apples, pears and plums and trugs of marrows, cauliflowers and onions — these are the essence of harvest festival decoration.

This arrangement is planned from the topmost flower to the lowest tip, in a gentle, flowing line. As gifts from members of the congregation are placed at the foot — a pot of honey, a bottle of fruit, a flower posy — they become a natural part of the design, simply extending the easy curves.

Mellow fruitfulness

A wide, deep willow basket is the perfect support for an offering of flowers, cereals and foliage. The autumnal flowers are bronze spider chrysanthemums, single spray chrysanthemums in apricot, bronze, red and white, coral alstroemeria, marigolds and dried achillea and Chinese lanterns.

Line the basket with something to give height — bricks for example — and place an old baking dish on top. Stand two blocks of soaked foam on end in the lefthand side of the dish. Crumple a piece of chicken wire over the foam and lay it flat across the rest of the dish. Tie it to the handles and fill the dish with water.

Step 1 Arrange the spray chrysanthemums in graded heights.
Step 2 Between them, insert stems of alstroemeria, achillea and opened-out Chinese lanterns. To open out Chinese lanterns, make four cuts in the seed cases and open them out like petals to reveal the richly coloured seeds. Arrange short alstroemeria stems and ivy leaves to conceal the foam. Fill in the design with oats, wheat, barley, grasses and teazels.
Step 3 Bind posies of marigolds and push some through the wire mesh into the water. Hang others from the basket. Conceal any foam with foliage.

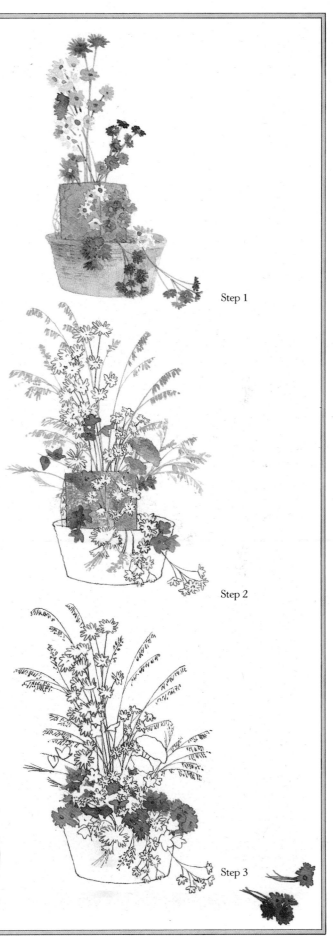

Step 1

Step 2

Step 3

EVERLASTING BEAUTY

Not only for those awkward times of year when the choice of fresh flowers is limited, but because you will learn to love their subtle tones and complex textures, dried and preserved plant materials form an important feature of the flower arranger's materials. With several preserving methods to choose from there are varied effects to be had, all equally beautiful and long-lasting.

The autumnal shades of coppery, glycerined beech leaves, grey-brown hydrangea heads, beige seedheads and faded grasses are familiar components, but by preserving summer flowers in desiccants you can add soft blues, pinks and mauves to your collection. Combine these with the brighter shades of the well-loved everlasting flowers and you have a considerable variety to mix and match.

Some preserved materials are very delicate, and it pays to acquire a few tricks – creating false stems and wiring heavy cones – so that stemless items need not be discarded. Try skeletonizing fleshy leaves or bleaching long stems of foliage, to add to the range of colours and textures.

Small, paper-dry and daisy-white everlasting flowers such as pearl, helipterum and ammobium; long and stately spikes of deepest blue delphinium and fiery golden rod; delicate parchment-coloured grasses, and tightly-packed heads of pink or blue hydrangea, these can all be preserved, almost for ever after, by the simplest means of all — they need only hang or stand in a free circulation of air.

Air-drying

All the everlasting flowers, also known as immortelles, are dried in this way. Others include single and double helichrysum, so cheerful in all the sunshine colours, everlasting pearl and statice, or sea lavender. Everlasting pearl may be bought dyed pink (see page 87), or you can dip them in commercial dye or red ink solution.

Apart from these, most of the flowers which dry satisfactorily by this method are those composed of a mass of tiny florets or flowers in a ball or umbrella shape, or clustered along a tall stem — mimosa, chives, onion and garlic, achillea, gypsophila, love-lies-bleeding, buddleia, marjoram, larkspur and clarkia and varied examples.

Grasses such as quaking grass (*Briza maxima*) and hare's tail (*Lagurus ovatus*) and seedheads of all kinds dry perfectly; in their soft, neutral shades they present a useful foil to the brightly coloured flowers. Long stems of lupin seedpods, like little dark grey velvet bolsters, the various urn shapes of poppy, love-in-a-mist and columbine, the pretty stars of mallow, and the dainty umbrellas of fennel, dill and caraway are all treasures far too pretty to banish to the compost heap.

Harvest all plant materials on a dry, warm day when there is the minimum of moisture in the air. Cut the stems as long as possible, but never pull or pluck them and risk damaging the plants. Harvest daisy-shaped everlasting flowers when the centres are just beginning to open; statice once it is fully open. Delphinium, clarkia and similar tall stems are at their best when a few of the lower flowers are in full bloom and some of the topmost buds are still tightly closed.

Grasses, rushes and cereals such as wheat, barley and oats should be cut when the flowers are just opening. The long, warm brown spikes of bulrushes, which give such positive lines to large arrangements, must be cut when they are very young and still have a long, stick-like strip at the top. Avoid handling the furry part and to prevent it from exploding, spray it with hair lacquer.

In good weather conditions you can leave seedheads to dry on the plants, but you can cut them and bring them indoors to mature and dry. Chinese lanterns (*Physalis franchetii*) are usually cut when they are turning deep orange. It is a good idea to leave a few stems on the plants in the hope that the pods will skeletonize naturally, revealing the large (and bitter) fruit inside a lace-like cage.

Preparation

Strip all leaves from the stems. In most cases it is a matter of choice whether you dry the materials by hanging them upside-down, or standing them upright in a container. If the stems are weak or the flowers top heavy they should be hung. You need a cool, dry, airy room that can be protected from strong light — steamy rooms and damp sheds will not do. A rope line, a ceiling beam, clothes hangers on wall hooks or an airing rack are suitable for hang-drying. For upright-drying use wide-necked crocks, bins or preserving jars, or pinholders, dry foam, or balls of holding clay pressed on to a base.

For hang-drying, tie stems into small bunches so that the flowers are not squashed — very large flowers should be dried singly. Use strong twine or raffia and make slip-knots that can easily be tightened as the stems dry. In upright drying, arrange the stems so that air can circulate all round the flowers.

Leave the materials to dry for at least one week; the larger the flower the longer the drying process, and it can sometimes take three weeks. The materials are ready when they rustle like tissue paper.

Some flowers, such as clarkia, delphinium and larkspur, benefit from being dried quickly in hot air, as they are more likely to retain their colour. Make sure that each flower is separated and hang them in bunches or spread them on racks in an airing cupboard or above a boiler. The flowers should be dry within two or three days. Rosebuds may also be dried in this way, but do not expect the same results as are achieved by commercial drying in heat-controlled chambers.

The flowers opposite, gathered from a summer's garden and simply dried by the air method, are shown on pages 88, 89 and 90 arranged in colourful displays.

LARKSPUR

LOVE-IN-A-MIST
SEEDHEADS

WILD
GARLIC
SEED-
HEADS

POPPY SEEDHEAD

DELPHINIUM

STATICE SUWOROWII

LARKSPUR

HELIPTERUM

WINGED
EVERLASTING
AMMOBIUM ALATUM
GRANDIFLORUM

MARJORAM

ROSEBUDS

HELICHRYSUM

EVERLASTING PEARL,
dyed pink and natural

STATICE LIMONIUM
SINUATUM

Storage

Sometimes the stems of dried flowers become too brittle and snap off — helichrysum are particularly guilty of this failing. If this happens, give the flowerhead a false stem of wire or straw (see below right).

Store dried materials in a dry room away from the light, which could cause fading. You can leave them hanging in bunches and upright in containers or, if it is more convenient, arrange them flat on racks or loosely packed in boxes.

To prevent mould growth, paint the stems with clear varnish, especially if you plan to arrange them with fresh flowers in water.

Arranging

Dried flowers look delicate and pretty arranged in baskets (above). A wooden trug, woven rush bowl, copper, brass or silver jug, bowl and candlestick, antique wooden tea caddy, white or painted china cup and saucer or a glass container, each provide a pleasing complement to the materials. The choice is endless when you arrange only dried flowers, for the container does not need to hold water.

Place dried flower arrangements away from strong sunlight. Inevitably they will fade a little in time, though sometimes a slight softening of the colours is due to nothing more permanent than dust! In that case, take them to the window and blow them with a hair dryer for a few seconds at the lowest setting (or else hold far away). It works wonders!

Making false stems

A dried flower stem that is brittle or too soft can be reinforced with wire, or a strong wheat or grass stalk. You can also replace the stem completely or lengthen stems that are too short. Use stub wires — 0.90mm (20 gauge) and 25cm (10 in) long is a good average strength to choose.

To strengthen or lengthen a hollow stem, push a wire right through it and into the flowerhead (fig 1). Alternatively, you could push the stem itself into a hollow wheat stalk.

If the flower has a feeble stem, or none at all, make a hook 5cm (2 in) from one end of the wire and push it through the flower from the top (fig 2). Bury the wire loop in the flower centre to hide it. Twist the two wire ends together beneath the flower, taking them round the stem if there is one. To camouflage wire stems, bind them from the top for about half their length with florist's adhesive tape (gutta percha) in brown or green, or use narrow strips of crepe paper.

Wiring cones

Dried cones add depth of colour and variety of texture to autumn and winter arrangements, garlands and decorative swags.

To wire the cones, use a 0.9mm (20 gauge) stub wire. Wind the wire round the cone above the lowest layer of scales, bring the two ends together and twist them neatly (fig 3).

fig 1

fig 2

fig 3

A mass of colourful dried flowers clustered into a basket is one of the prettiest lasting reminders of summer. Tiny gypsy baskets filled with pink and white everlasting flowers make charming dressing-table decorations and unusual 'bouquets' for young bridesmaids — romantic keepsakes after the wedding, too. A large flower-filled basket brightens an empty fireplace all year round with dancing-flame colours, or make a trailing arrangement with long sprays of dried blooms, to hang in a hall, porch or room corner. Simple sprays of mixed dried flowers look good as wall decorations and make thoughtful and long-lasting gifts for friends who have no garden.

Holding material

If a basket is likely to be vulnerable and easily knocked over, weight it down with a few washed stones. Wedge a piece of dry plastic foam into the basket just rising above the neck. If it does not fit tightly, tie fine twine around the basket handles from side to side.

Selecting the flowers

For the bouquet of mixed flowers intended to be hung on a wall, the same guidelines apply for the selection of both fresh and dried flowers. (See page 65 for more detailed information.)

In the arrangements shown here, so apparently casual and natural, the effect is achieved only by a careful choice of the materials. Both the small and the large baskets have a mixture of long, spiky stems forming the outline and flat, round-faced flowers providing emphasis and focal points. Sprays of minute flowers, green *Alchemilla mollis* and white gypsophila, give a pretty veiling effect, especially when they overlap large heads of achillea and hydrangea. When a wide variety of materials is used, colour harmony is especially important — whether it is mainly pink, mauve and white with touches of golden yellow, or spans the range of cream, orange and yellow, as in our examples on these pages.

Arranging the flowers

For the small baskets, cut short stems so that the arrangement will make a rounded cushion shape and leave the handles clear.

Arrange the statice and lavender, which act as both side points and fillers, and then place the pink and white helipterum as scattered highlights. Tiny sprays of *Alchemilla mollis* arranged last, fill the remaining spaces.

Both these large baskets are designed to stand on the floor and so will be viewed from above. Therefore it is a good idea to place the baskets on a low table when you start work.

To make the arrangement shown at the top of the facing page, first position the side sprays of love-lies-bleeding, clarkia, delphinium and statice. Then add the large heads of achillea and, an unusual touch, sprays of pink silk flowers. Fill up the design with helipterum, statice, gypsophila and *Alchemilla mollis*. Check from each side that the foam is completely hidden.

To make the large basket arrangement shown below, start arranging from the centre and work towards the sides. Begin by positioning the hydrangea, achillea and Chinese lanterns. Keeping a neat shape, position the outline stems of yellow and white statice, and fill in with gypsophila and *Alchemilla mollis*.

A SHEAF OF DRIED FLOWERS

Sugar-icing pink and parchment cream, mint green and deep, deep purple, sunshine gold and velvety red, harvest corn and sparkling white, are the romantic and pretty colours of this dried flower sheaf wall decoration. You may already have all the ingredients you need to make a similar sheaf — almost any mixture of dried materials will make a lovely decoration. Or you can make it a long-term project, collecting and drying the flowers, seedheads and grasses throughout the year and tying them into small bunches. When you have enough, you simply bring them together to make the prettiest-ever wall hanging.

We used a mixture of dried flowers, seed pods, grasses and cereals. Make your own selection, according to availability, choosing long spiky flowers and grasses for the base and graduating to small, round-faced flowers at the top. A small flower posy was wired to the top-most stems of this arrangement, just beneath the ribbon bow, to add a special touch.

A dried flower sheaf

Step 1 Arrange three long bunches on the table to form a fan shape for the base. Bind them securely together with silver roll wire.

Step 2 Arrange two more bunches on each side to increase the width, and wire them in place.

Step 3 Working towards the stem end, cover the stems with bunches of shorter materials, binding each one firmly in place.

Step 4 Make a posy of everlasting flowers and bind it to the stems at the top. Finish the sheaf by wrapping the stems with ribbon.

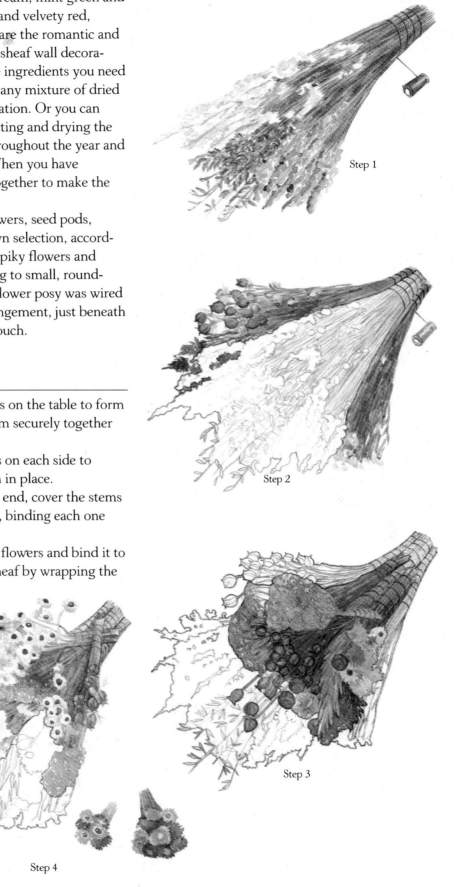

Step 1

Step 2

Step 3

Step 4

You can add more dried flowers to your collection by treating them in a powder. This method is known as drying in desiccants; the flowers are closely packed in the drying medium, which gradually draws the moisture from the petals and leaves the flowers in perfect shape. Flowers dried by this method have a less shrivelled look than those preserved by air-drying and it is suitable for a wider range of materials.

Use desiccants to preserve single, flat-faced flowers — buttercups, daisies, primulas and pansies, double- and multi-petalled flowers such as zinnias and carnations, and short sprays of bell-shaped flowers — lily-of-the-valley, hyacinth and forsythia. Perhaps prettiest of all are roses, dried in tight bud or partly open.

Suitable desiccants are household borax and alum (either separately or in a mixture of equal parts) which can be used for the most delicate of flowers, even violets; silica gel crystals ground in powder form can be used for medium and large flowers and builder's sand, washed and thoroughly dried, for the largest specimens. You can buy borax, alum and silica gel from chemists, of which silica gel is the most expensive. All desiccants can be dried in a cool oven after use and stored in airtight jars.

Drying by desiccants

Select an airtight container, no longer used for storing food, such as an old biscuit tin, or a box made from polythene, wood or strong cardboard. Cover the base with a layer of powder 2.5cm (1 in) deep. Cut the flower stems to about 2.5cm (1 in) long and push the stems separately into the desiccant so that the flowers are resting face up on the powder, not touching each other. Lay sprays of flowers (larkspur or jasmine, for example) on top of the powder, again not touching each other (fig 1).

Sprinkle on more powder, filtering it with your hand (fig 2) and making sure that it is in close contact with every surface of every petal. Cover the flowers with a 2.5cm (1 in) layer, put the lid on the container and, if necessary, seal it with sticky tape to make it airtight.

Leave the box undisturbed in a warm, dry room until the flowers are dry and crisp, which takes from four to fourteen days, according to size.

Stems and storage

Carefully lift out the flowers and dust off the powder with a small camelhair paintbrush. To make the dried flowers less fragile and to give them a semi-matt 'bloom', spray them with hair lacquer or artists' fixative. Insert false stems, using wire or natural stalks (see page 88). Store the flowers upright with the stalks pushed into a block of foam (fig 3) or pack them in a box between tissues.

The lattice bowl

A shallow white pottery bowl is a sparkling container for summer flowers (opposite), which can be preserved either by air-drying (see page 86) or in desiccants (this page). Rosebuds are more satisfactory if dried in desiccants, but the long flower spikes — larkspur, delphiniums and clarkia — can only be preserved by this method if cut into short sprays.

Crumple a piece of wire netting to about the size of a fist, place it towards the back of the bowl and tie it to the rim to keep it from sliding. Arrange spikes of larkspur, clarkia, delphinium and statice so that the stems are held firmly in the netting. Place love-in-a-mist seedheads and the everlasting flowers amongst them. Finally add rosebuds, the most beautiful and fragile of them all.

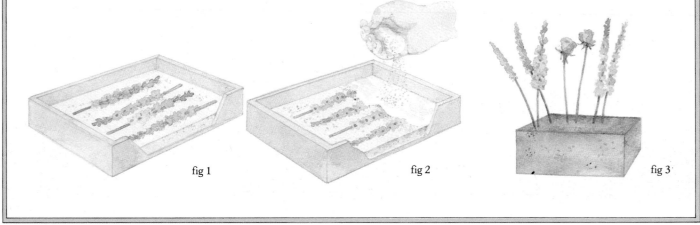

fig 1   fig 2   fig 3

A LATTICE BOWL ARRANGEMENT

The three methods of preservation described on this page produce effects as different from each other as the lustre in a spray of glycerined leaves and berries is from the paper-crisp texture of hydrangea heads dried in water, or the intricate lace-like patterns of skeletonized magnolia leaves.

The glycerine method

Whereas air- and powder-drying take the moisture from plant materials, leaving them dry and papery, glycerine is absorbed by the plants, so they remain flexible and lifelike.

This method of preserving is suitable for sprays of deciduous leaves — beech are the most familiar — and large, separate leaves such as fig; evergreens of all types; fruits such as rosehips and blackberries; columns of flowers like foxgloves and Bells of Ireland bracts, illustrated opposite.

Gather leaves of deciduous plants in midsummer, while they are still absorbing moisture; evergreens can be preserved at any time. Strip off lower leaves and pare away bark from woody stem ends, which should be lightly crushed or split.

Mix one part glycerine with two parts very hot water and stir the mixture vigorously. Pour it into a heatproof container — an old vase or preserving jar is ideal — to a depth of 5cm (2 in). Stand the stems in the solution (fig 1) and place the jar with foliage in a cool, dark room until the leaves have changed colour. Most take on deep, autumnal tints and some, like laurel, turn almost black. Light-weight foliage might be ready in one week, tough leaves might take up to eight weeks.

Very large, robust leaves — fig, *Fatsia japonica* and bergenia — are best immersed singly in a shallow dish of the solution (fig 2).

Wipe the preserved leaves with a damp tissue and dry the stems. Spray berries with hair lacquer. Store preserved materials upright in containers, hanging in bunches or loosely packed in boxes.

Water drying

This might seem a contradiction of terms, but this is the most suitable method for preserving shrubby plants with tough stems, and for some thick-centred flowers. These include hydrangeas (as an alternative method to air-drying) and heathers, *Chrysanthemum parthenium* and double zinnias.

Cut the flowers when they have started to dry on the plant. Stand the stems in about 12mm (½ in) of cold water and leave them, without topping up the water, until it has been absorbed. Wipe the stems dry.

Skeletonizing

This is the process by which the leaf tissue is stripped off, revealing the lace-like leaf structure. It is suitable for fleshy evergreen leaves such as holly, ivy, magnolia and laurel and, indeed, occurs naturally. Treated leaves are especially pretty with dried flowers, and can be sprayed with metallic or coloured paints.

In a large, old saucepan bring to the boil 1 litre (1¾ pints) water and 250g (8 oz) blue household detergent powder. Add the leaves and boil them for 30 minutes. Rinse them under cold water, then scrub off the leaf tissue with a stiff brush — an old toothbrush will do (fig 3). Dry the leaves between blotting paper and press them with an iron. Store the pressed leaves in boxes between tissues.

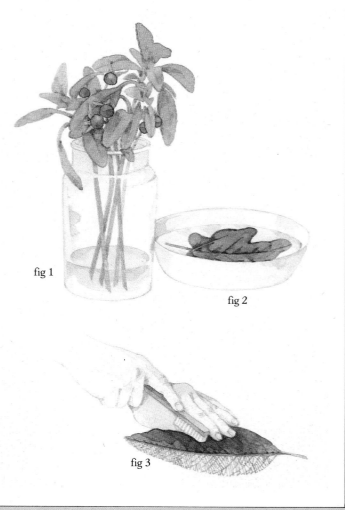

fig 1

fig 2

fig 3

ROSE HIPS

CUPRESSUS

BAY LEAVES

TWIGS WITH
DRIED CONES

YELLOW HOLLY

BLACKBERRY LEAVES

HOLLY with berries

BEECH LEAVES

BELLS OF IRELAND,
glycerined and bleached

IVY LEAVES

MAHONIA LEAVES, glycerined

MAHONIA LEAVES, untreated

EUCALYPTUS
glycerined and bleached

A collection of plant materials preserved in all the
golden and brown hues of autumn can be sup-
plemented with dried or fresh flowers for extra colour.
When water or soaked holding foam is needed for
fresh materials, paint the stems and stem ends of
preserved material with clear varnish or lacquer and
leave them to dry. This will prevent mould forming on
contact with moisture.

The 'golden-glow' arrangement (opposite) combines
preserved leaves, hips and flower bracts with dried
cones and dried rosebuds. You can see all these items
in close-up on page 95.

An autumn arrangement

The container is a long, narrow wooden basket with a
sturdy, bentwood handle. A block of dry (grey) holding
foam on the left is tied, parcelwise, to the handles.

Step 1 Position the bleached eucalyptus leaves at the
back and sides, then the beech leaves and rose hips that
follow the same lines. Add the mahonia leaf on the left,
the twigs of cones on the right, and the Bells of Ireland
bracts.

Step 2 Make a 'nest' of blackberry, holly, cupressus and
bay leaves at the centre front, making sure the foam is
completely covered. Arrange the leaves so that the
various colours are separated, from the lighter green of
the holly to the bronze-red of the blackberry.

Step 3 Arrange short stems of rose hips at the front and
between them the dried rose buds. Handle these
delicate flowers very carefully as they are easily
crushed.

Sun bleaching

To achieve the beautiful pale parchment effect of the
eucalyptus leaves and Bells of Ireland bracts in the
arrangement, simply hang them in direct sunlight.
Stand the materials in the glycerine solution for only
four days. Take them out, wipe the stems dry and tie
them in bunches. Hang them in a window in strong
sunshine – this could prove the greatest difficulty! —
for a week or so, until they are thoroughly bleached.

Apply the sun bleaching treatment to trailing ivy
sprays, holly, beech and laurel stems, or large, single
leaves of fatsia and aspidistra. They will all fade to
attractive creamy tones useful for high contrast.

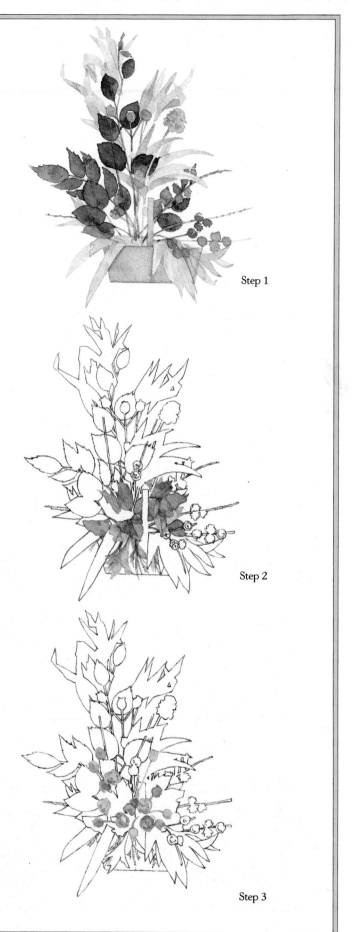

Step 1

Step 2

Step 3

AN AUTUMN ARRANGEMENT

CONTAINERS & EQUIPMENT

*F*lowers are the focus of attention, but they are only one component of a successful flower arrangement. The choice of container can make or break a design from the start – and there are many unseen aids to a natural-looking display. No 'cheating' is involved – simply the materials and equipment of the craft, as required by all artists and designers, whatever the discipline.

You may find one simple white vase endlessly useful, adapting easily to formal or casual arrangements. Experiments with a variety of containers, however, will prove how they can enhance a design and even provide the basic inspiration. With the use of holding equipment – water-retaining foam, pinholders and wire netting, and judicious use of fixers, such as wire and adhesive clay – you can greatly extend the potential of a group of plant materials.

What do Granny's old coffee pot, a wooden cheese board, a seashell, a brass preserving pan and a souvenir mug have in common? The answer is that all these items, and many more you might have around the home, can be used as containers for fresh and preserved flowers. In fact, almost any ornament or household item, whether it is old or new, hollow or flat, capable of holding water or not, can be used to contain or display plant materials.

Containers may be visually pleasing, forming a partnership with the flowers and leaves, or simply functional. Strictly utilitarian containers might be chosen only because they are the right height for an alcove or the exact width needed for a windowsill, and will be concealed by the plant materials.

There is an enormous range of purpose-made flower containers in pottery, china, glass and plastic, and everyone who enjoys arranging flowers is sure to have quite a collection. Surprisingly, however, it is often the more off-beat items or pieces designed for a quite different function that become favourites.

By considering the different seasonal plant materials, the designs you enjoy creating and the variety of moods and occasions they represent, you can form an idea of the range of containers it is useful to have on hand. You will soon develop a keen eye for likely candidates at jumble sales or on the 'seconds' stall. A hot water jug and matching bowl with chipped rims might disappoint the antiques bargain hunter but, as every flower arranger knows, a well-placed leaf can hide a multitude of imperfections, and paired items like these give extra scope for ingenuity.

Baskets are 'naturals'

Generally, unpretentious containers in soft, muted colours are the best choice for the new enthusiast. Baskets have a special affinity with flowers, and look most charming with spring blooms, wild flowers, or an informal handful of garden flowers. A lidded basket brimming over with the first precious primroses, a garden trug or basket crammed with marguerites and studded with poppies to stand in the fireplace, a silvered basket filled with roses for a christening, a bread basket as the base for a table centrepiece — the designs almost suggest themselves.

To arrange fresh flowers in a basket or other non-waterproof container, line it first with polythene or foil and wedge in a block of soaked plastic foam, or place a smaller watertight container inside.

Upright containers are useful for apparently artless displays in which the flowers are arranged without any holding material. Look beyond the obvious possibilities of pottery, china and glass vases to jugs, mugs, storage and cosmetic jars and tea tins.

You can treat a patterned container in two ways. Either match the flower colours exactly to the design, or choose a single colour in harmony or contrast. A lustre teapot could be filled with a profusion of blue, pink and white flowers for an 'Old Masters' look, or with a striking display of plain red tulips.

When upright containers are fitted with foam at the neck, they become, in effect, pedestals and can then support more formal curves, cascades and trailing designs which are perfect for a buffet table or tall alcove. Footed cake stands, fruit bowls and urns already have a pedestal form.

To improvise upright containers, which can be concealed by trailing plant sprays, you can use painted coffee jars, food cans or even plastic washing-up liquid bottles, partly filled with sand to weight the base. When you are searching for a narrow container for a church windowsill or a huge one for the harvest festival, you can paint household items such as an old loaf tin or a garden bucket. Use a matt paint in a quiet colour — cream, stone, brown or sage green.

Shallow dishes make versatile containers especially suited to vertical, horizontal and right-angled designs. A brown earthenware baking dish with russet-coloured autumnal flowers, a white fluted flan dish with cornflowers and yellow alstromeria, a glass dish with silver foliage and pink roses — the partnerships are endless. For a cool effect, particularly refreshing in the summer, fix a pinholder at one side of the dish only, so the flowers rise beside a pool of water.

Wood is wonderful

Wooden boards, trays and boxes are invaluable for arrangements of dried and preserved materials and, with a concealed inner container, are equally well-matched to fresh flowers. Cheeseboards, pencil trays, well-scrubbed seed trays, filing boxes, round cheese box lids begged from the delicatessen, wicker place mats, bamboo trays and tea caddies all have possibilities as suitable containers.

Look, no stalks! A plastic foam-holder topping the pierced pottery stand, left, holds stems of godetia, sweet pea and euphorbia.

A seashell, below left, filled with foam gives the colour cue for a small, formal design of two-tone pinks, everlasting peas and ballota leaves.

Glistening glass, below right, makes a neutral but sparkling stand for freesias and double narcissi.

Snowdrops, above, are supported by a pinholder in a shallow dish.

The miniature dairy-can, far right, holds wild roses, blackberry blossom and strawberry leaves.

A rustic basket, right, is a natural complement to wheat, oats and poppies.

Smaller items can be fitted with holding clay and decorated with dried flowers to make novel gifts. A wooden kitchen spoon with a posy of dried flowers and a ribbon bow, an egg cup with a candle-shaped burst of seedheads, a date box topped with vibrant helichrysums; these can all be assembled in moments and will give pleasure for months.

The glitter of metal adds richness to flowers of all seasons — daffodils in a pewter jug, wild roses in a silver bowl, dahlias in a copper tankard, evergreens and berries in a brass preserving pan. Wash, dry and clean metal containers thoroughly before storage.

Natural materials make pretty flower holders — seashells surrounding preserved or fresh flowers; dried flowers glued to a pine-cone; eggshells with violets and primroses. Driftwood can be so placed in an arrangement that flowers appear to be growing around it. Pieces of granite make perfect bases — stunning with sea holly and statice — and pebbles, stones and gravel are practised in the art of disguising mechanics.

Much of the enjoyment of flower arranging is in choosing the container. A thimble for a miniature design, a brass warming pan for winter berries, a sauceboat and stand for a table decoration, a blackened saucepan or large earthenware pot for an outdoor party — once you start on your treasure hunt, nothing in the home is sacred!

Small round or rectangular wicker baskets are traditional containers for spring primroses, violets, grape hyacinths or snowdrops. Line the basket with a water-holding container and use a pinholder or crumpled netting to support the slender and fragile stems. For thicker stems, a block of soaked foam is suitable.

A shallow baking dish, whatever its shape, can be the base for symmetrical, triangular, horizontal, vertical and L-shaped designs. It is particularly suited to off-centre designs for competitions in which the water is a feature of the theme.

Candlesticks — press a ball of modelling compound on to a candlestick to hold stems of cereals, seedheads, grasses and dried flowers. A group of three holders makes an unusual and long-lasting table decoration.

Tankards, mugs and beakers can be used for loose, upright arrangements, or can be filled with foam or wire netting. They are best suited to informal groups of wild or garden flowers.

A wide, deep fruit bowl can support a large symmetrical arrangement of flowers, or a winter design of evergreens, berries and fruit. Fit the bowl with a high-standing block of foam covered with wire netting.

Matching items from a dinner or tea service lend perfect harmony as containers for the table centre — a sugar bowl and jug, teapot, cup and saucer or even a casserole are among the possibilities.

Large seashells, which you can buy quite cheaply at souvenir shops, are sympathetic containers for both dried and fresh flowers. Fill the cavity with plastic foam and arrange a tumbling profusion of plant material to resemble a 'horn of plenty'.

Copper containers — the glint of metal is flattering to flowers of all seasons. A copper tea caddy with a narrow neck is attractively filled with a few stems of evergreens and berries. Fitted with a saucer holder and foam, it comes to life with the addition of flame-coloured dahlias, zinnias or rudbeckia.

A plain cylinder vase never distracts from the flowers and is equally suited to a handful of white marguerites or a nosegay of mixed summer blooms. Simplicity often equals beauty in flower arranging.

Teapots and coffee pots, which have seen better days, are some of the best bargains at jumble sales. Match the flowers to colours in the pattern, or highlight just one of the colours.

Urn-shaped vases come in many materials and sizes, from a small vase with blue and white Wedgwood pattern to a large, eye-catching white pot. According to the scale of the material, you can use foam and crumpled wire netting, separately or together, as stemholders.

A loaf tin filled with wire netting and painted matt cream is a good example of a container that is more useful than decorative. It is particularly suited to an arrangement for a narrow niche or windowsill where they can be disguised with foliage.

Every keen flower arranger will slowly acquire, as well as a collection of versatile containers, a stock of mechanics and equipment to make the task easier and provide for more varied designs.

You have only to mention the word 'mechanics' to some people for them to say, 'Oh, I couldn't possibly use those. And anyway, I prefer flowers to look natural', as if by the introduction of a simple stem-holder every flower is going to be forced into an unnatural attitude. These people have the wrong idea of 'mechanics'.

It is in fact much more limiting to make a pleasing arrangement without any holding material. To do so you have to find a container of exactly the right dimensions and this rigid requirement eliminates any number of exciting possibilities.

To cut stems

Before examining the benefits of wire and holders, it is important to realise that stems must be properly prepared. Cut all stems neatly and cleanly, without damage to either plant or cutters. Kitchen scissors are unreliable, so buy a good pair of floral secateurs and check that they feel comfortable. Set aside a sharp kitchen knife or penknife to scrape bark and slit stems and a pair of small scissors to cut off unwanted leaves.

To wire stems

If you are making bouquets, formal posies and swags — and many other designs besides — you will find stub wires invaluable. These are used to lengthen, strengthen or replace stems, to increase flexibility in some and to tame others (such as tulips), to bind posies and to attach plant materials to a rope for swag designs. Rolls of fine silver wire — fuse wire will do — are useful for posies and swags, and for securing holding materials to a container.

Stub wires are available from florists' suppliers, in lengths from 90mm (3½ in) to 460mm (18 in) and in thicknesses varying from 1.25mm (18 gauge) to 0.20 mm (36 gauge). Fine and medium grades are most useful. Store the wires in a plastic bag smeared with vegetable oil or petroleum jelly — or with a few silica gel crystals — so they are less likely to rust.

Include in your kit a pair of wire cutters. Those with a notched wheel attached to handle grips are best.

To hide the unfriendly appearance of wire stems you will need a roll of florist's tape. It is called gutta percha and is available in brown or green.

To hold stems

The most useful means of holding stems are blocks of plastic foam, crumpled wire netting and pinholders. Other materials such as marbles, pebbles and modelling compound or adhesive clay have more specific and limited uses.

Plastic foam blocks are available in two types. One is for use with dried and preserved materials and is always used dry, the other, for fresh materials, retains moisture when soaked in water. Both types are available in two sizes from florists, cylinders about 7.5cm (3 in) in diameter and 6cm (2¼ in) deep, and rectangles about 24 × 12cm (9 × 4½ in) and 7.5cm (3 in) deep. They can be used whole or cut to fit a container.

Soak the moisture-retaining type in water for 15 to 20 minutes before use, and keep it topped up with water as long as the arrangement lasts. Afterwards, store it damp in a sealed plastic bag. Foam blocks can be re-used if they are not allowed to dry.

Foam blocks have a wide variety of uses. The main advantages are that they hold stems in place at any angle, and enable you to make use of the most unlikely containers.

If a block of foam is cut to extend well above the rim of a container, it is possible to place stems at an angle so that they trail downwards over a pedestal or in a cascade design. In low, flat styles of arrangement, the foam holds the stem horizontally.

Fresh flowers can be arranged in soaked foam blocks to protect containers of silver or crystal, for example, from being scratched by woody stems. Foam is invaluable if the container has an awkward shape — a seashell, wall vase, or a heart-shaped tin which you might use for a Valentine or engagement party.

Containers with very narrow necks such as wine bottles and flasks, or with no aperture at all, like candlesticks, can be fitted with a cylinder of foam to hold a profusion of stems.

To fix the foam securely to a tall container or on a wooden board, you can wedge it into an upturned coffee-jar lid or, more satisfactory, a plastic 'saucer' designed to fit the cylinder exactly (see fig 1, page 105). Use silver wire to secure the holder to the neck of the container. To fit into the tops of bottles there are 'candlecup' holders with a plug base to fit into a bottleneck (see fig 7, page 105).

If a foam block is to hold heavy, woody stems or large flowers it needs extra support or it may crumble. Cover the foam with 5cm (2 in) galvanized wire netting, crumpled into shape and wired firmly to the container. You can buy this netting by the metre from garden supply shops. Cut off the doubled, sealed edge, and it is ready for use. Crumpled wire alone is an effective stem holder in wide, open containers such as bowls and tureens. Cut the wire to about three times the size of the aperture and crush it in your hands. Push it into the neck to form a dome shape and wire it in place if necessary.

Sometimes a pinholder may be needed in conjunction with wire netting, to anchor heavy stems more

firmly (fig 1). The best pinholders are heavy lead bases and long metal pins; they are available in a range of sizes. You can fix a pinholder in a shallow water-holding container, on a board or in a shallow dish, for example, or buy a 'well' holder in which the pins are set into a deep cylinder.

Glass marbles and pebbles are effective stem-holders, especially in glass containers. Balls of modelling compound pressed on to, for example, a figurine or piece of driftwood hold stems of preserved material. Wooden cocktail sticks are useful to impale fruit.

To give a firm foundation

It is essential that pinholders, foam saucers and other such items that act as concealed or inner containers are firmly anchored. Make sure all the items are absolutely dry, and press small balls of modelling compound or adhesive clay to the holder. Twist it back and forth on the container until the clay takes a firm grip.

To carry moisture

For very large designs, a pedestal arrangement in church or on a stage, perhaps, it is often necessary to construct a concealed source of water for stems which cannot reach into the container or base of soaked foam. In this way the height of a design can be greatly increased, or short-stemmed flowers can be given, as it were, stilts and a drink at the same time! You can buy small cone-shaped florist's funnels for the purpose, some already attached to a fine stick (fig 2). Or improvise by cutting off the tightly-screwed top of a plastic bottle, making an almost conical shape, or using a plastic toothbrush holder. Another way round the situation is to bind a piece of soaked foam to a thin strip of cane, and pierce the stems into that.

You will also need a florist's watering-can with a long spout (fig 3), to top up the water in arrangements and fill narrow-necked containers, and a fine atomizer spray to sprinkle flowers and foliage with water, to keep them cool and fresh.

Finally, always have on hand a large sheet of polythene to cover table, floor and other working surfaces. You can gather it up by the corners and shoot all the trimmings on to the compost heap or into the dustbin. But check first to make sure that your secateurs and scissors don't go with them!

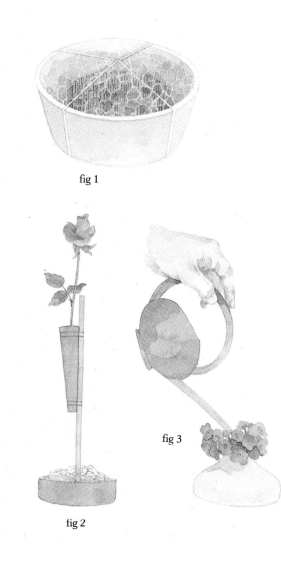

fig 1

fig 3

fig 2

A specially made plastic 'saucer' (fig 1) has a recess at the centre which provides a secure hold on a cylinder of plastic foam. It can be used as the base for a small arrangement, or may be attached to a board or set in any one of a variety of containers.

A piece cut from a block of foam (fig 2) is wedged into a dish. To allow flowers to slant downwards, cut the foam to extend to an appropriate height above the rim.

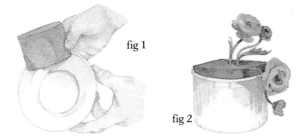

fig 1

fig 2

Heavy-based pinholders (fig 3) in a range of sizes are invaluable. Small ones support slender and fragile stems between the spikes, while thick, woody stems are impaled on the pins of large holders.

To be on the safe side, spend a little time securing all mechanics. Place small balls of adhesive clay on the base of a pinholder (fig 4) and press it on to the floor of the container. You can also use clay, as an alternative to wire, to fix plastic foam-holders into containers.

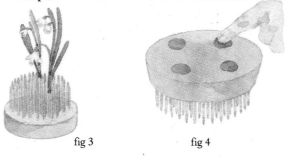

fig 3

fig 4

A pinholder firmly anchored in a water-holding container, and the dish secured to a board — clay is the adhesive in both cases. Here (fig 5) the mechanics are placed to one side so that the polished wood base forms an integral part of the design.

fig 5

When crumpled wire netting is fitted into the neck of a tall container, a pinholder can form a useful anchor in the base, to secure heavy stems. This illustration (fig 6) shows how the same combination can be used in a shallow container. The stems are pushed through the netting and on to the pinholder. For extra security, twist the cut ends of the wire around the stems.

Plastic or metal 'candlecups' are made with a plug at the base, to fit securely into the neck of a bottle or candlestick. Even so, it is advisable to press a ring of adhesive clay around the plug, for extra strength (fig 7). The 'cup' can be fitted with foam or chicken wire.

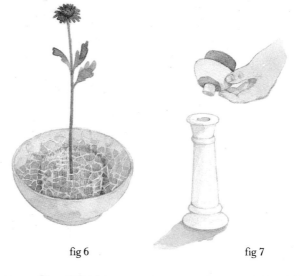

fig 6

fig 7

One roll of fine silver-coloured wire, such as fuse wire, and one of a slightly thicker gauge are useful for binding stems in bouquets and posies and securing the components of a swag. Bundles of stub wires in various grades are used to strengthen and replace stems, and also for binding (fig 8).

Every flower arranger needs the right tools for the job! Invest in a good pair of secateurs to cut stems cleanly — try them first for size, weight and grip — and a small pair of scissors to trim leaves (fig 9).

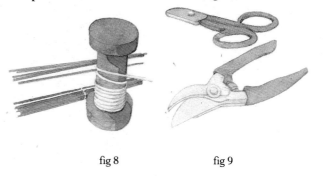

fig 8

fig 9

A-Z
IDEAL
PLANTS

*E*very flower and leaf in an arrangement
should make an essential contribution to the
overall design. You can be confident of a good
result, and avoid wasting plant materials, if
you select each item with a good idea of the
part it will play in the arrangement. This
chapter explains the basic shapes of flowers
and leaves and their place in flower arranging,
giving hints on which to pick and the right
stage of growth for cutting. Florists' flowers
can be expensive and of limited range; if you
have a garden you can organise the planting
to yield a wide selection suitable for many
different styles of arrangement.

    A fully illustrated A-Z is included here,
specially selected by an experienced arranger.
It is not a growing guide, nor is it a
comprehensive list, since many of the flowers
used throughout the book are familiar and
readily available. The A-Z is compiled to focus
on some less familiar plants and those which
are particularly recommended for flower
arranging. It gives basic information as to
where and when you can find them, their
colours and special features, and tips on the
care and conditioning of individual items, for
use in their fresh state and, as appropriate,
dried or preserved.

Plant materials fall into three basic groups, and most flower arrangements require a few of each sort.

Pointed You will generally need some slim, pointed shapes for making the outline or silhouette of an arrangement. Suitable items include the flowers and foliage of gladioli, lily spikes, wild dock or willow herb, delphinium spires, iris leaves, and sprays of beech. The buds of many flowers, such as the rose and the iris are of this same useful pointed shape. The trick of using the side view of round-faced blooms — dahlias, pinks, carnations, marigolds, or aquilegia — in the outline of an arrangement works in exactly the same way, leading the eye gently but firmly into the main part of the design. Sprays of privet leaves, ivy trails, ferns, lavender, flowering lime stripped of its leaves, all work exceptionally well as outline material and are much favoured by experienced arrangers.

Round Every arrangement needs a centre of interest, to draw the eye irresistibly and hold it for a moment at the heart of the design. For this important position you might well choose something rather round in shape, such as a perfect newly-opened rose just showing its centre, a houseleek rosette, a head of rhododendron or hydrangea, or the largest and most perfect peony in a bunch. A group of flowers closely packed, or a cluster of fruits or nuts are other strong and confident items for the 'focal point' of an arrangement.

Transitional To heighten the visual effect of the main area of interest, try surrounding it with a few plain, well-formed, semi-round shapes such as individual ivy leaves, hosta, or even beetroot or cabbage leaves. These will provide a quiet foil and set off the more flamboyant flowers to perfection. They help to link the pointed or spiky shapes of the outline and the rounder central flowers. Other items useful for filling in between the two extremes might be a number of half-open flowers, some oval-shaped fruits, flowers or leaves of medium size, or flowers placed in three-quarter view rather than full-face.

Some flowers grow with a most useful advantage to the arranger — they are very adaptable, having points, rounds, and semi-rounds built into their overall shape. Counted among these are lilies, gladioli, and hyacinths, which will effectively stand alone in a stylish arrangement with only a few accompanying leaves, but which will also slip equally happily into a mixed flower group. So when you are buying a few flowers, or picking them in the wild or from the garden, bear in mind the three basic categories of shape and how you will use them in the arrangement. Beginners will find it far easier to use a few varieties of plant material, with identifiable shapes, rather than a very diverse mix.

Which flowers to pick

When you come to think about it, it makes very good sense to pick or buy flowers at the perfect, close-to-opening bud stage or when they are only just opened. Avoid any blooms which may have been wide open for a day or more. Don't pick garden flowers if you know they are being, or have recently been, visited by bees — these will have a shortened life expectancy.

Flowers with double and semi-double petals will always last much longer than single-petalled blooms. It is worth remembering, too, that plants which grow with plenty of buds — to open slowly over a period — will have extra long life in an arrangement. All foliage should last longer than flowers, while sprays of berries, grasses, and seedheads in a wide variety will give pleasure for weeks, making an excellent backing for a constantly changing procession of flowers.

Some flowers by their very nature last much better than others. A bunch of chrysanthemums will always have greater staying power than a sheaf of daffodils; an orchid spray will last for weeks but a bunch of violets only for days. This is not to say one is more desirable in an arrangement than the other — a posy of violets may suit the mood of a winter afternoon more successfully than an orchid.

When you are wandering round the garden, gather flowers with thought specifically for a particular room or for the arrangement you have in mind, rather than dashing around enthusiastically picking willy-nilly whatever happens to take your fancy. Try working up a colour scheme as you go, picking only flowers or leaves which harmonize or contrast pleasantly. Don't pick more than you need. Choose some stems growing with a slight curve, to give a feeling of life and movement to the outline of your arrangement.

The size of flower or leaf is important. No-one, however skilled or experienced, is likely to achieve a really good decorative effect with a bunch of material made up of very diverse sizes — for example, one

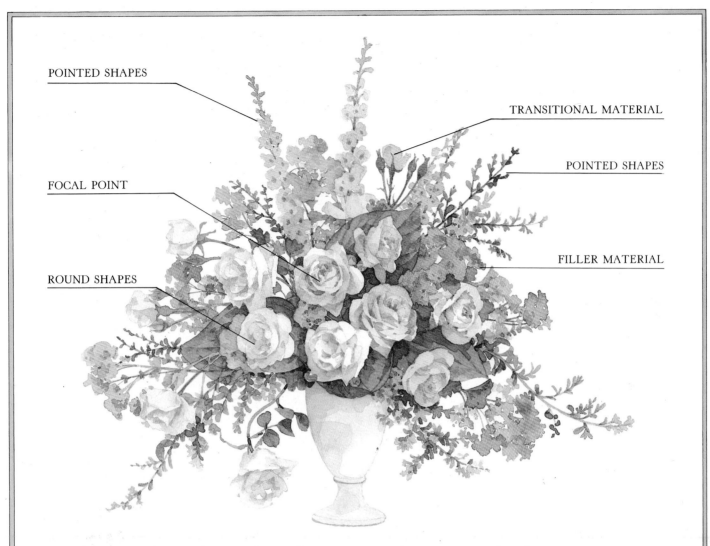

POINTED SHAPES

TRANSITIONAL MATERIAL

POINTED SHAPES

FOCAL POINT

FILLER MATERIAL

ROUND SHAPES

blowsy, cabbage-sized oriental poppy, four or five delicate-looking annual poppies, a couple of lupins, and a sprig or two of lavender will form an uneasy mixture. A more even match is much easier to arrange. To start with, one should decide between the big poppies and the smaller annual ones, gathering either one or the other, and taking some in tight bud, others fully-open, and some half-open. The lavender and lupins would not be necessary. This description is exaggerated to illustrate the basic problem. So often beginners pick or buy unsuitable mixtures and so make the whole task of arranging very difficult from the start.

Which flowers to grow

There are absolutely hundreds of plants which flower arrangers particularly like for cutting and it would be impossible to list them all. Here, however, are some you are likely to meet, plus a few more off-beat ones which can add to the interest of your garden and

contribute to many styles of arrangement.

A good collection of plant, seed, and bulb catalogues is truly invaluable and makes fascinating reading. It is worth sending away for them — and most are free!

NOTE the common terms which horticulturalists use to categorize different types of plants:

Annuals — plants for which seed is sown and flowers and fruits are picked in the same year, then the plant dies.
Biennials — plants for which seed is sown to obtain flowers or fruits the following year.
Perennials — plants which go on flowering or fruiting year after year.
Tender plants — those which are not frost-hardy.
Hardy plants — those which usually withstand normal winter temperatures in most parts of Britain.
Deciduous — shrub or tree which sheds its leaves annually at the end of the growing season.

Acacia
Mimosa
Small tree or large shrub

Colour Yellow flowers.
Available Winter to early spring from florists.
Cutting and preparation A difficult subject. Keep in plastic bag as long as possible to prevent shrivelling. Submerge whole flowerhead in cold water for a few minutes. Crush stem ends and give hot water drink. Florists often include a special powder for adding to water to stop blossoms shrivelling.
Remarks Well suited for drying in one of the desiccants, which retains the original fluffiness. Preserved flowers and leaves are useful for pressed flower pictures and decorations as well as for dried arrangements. Although it can be grown in Britain in a greenhouse or against a sheltered wall it is mostly available from florists.

Acroclinium or Helipterum
Straw daisy or Australian everlasting.
Grown in Britain as an annual

Colour Delicate pale rose, carmine, or white flowers.
Available Summer; preserve for winter use or buy dried from florists.
Cutting and preparation Pick some in bud, others recently opened, on warm sunny days. Strip away all leaves, dry by hanging.
Remarks Sow seed in May in open ground where the flowers are to bloom.

Alchemilla mollis
Lady's mantle
Hardy perennial

Colour Attractive lime green flowers, which dry green or soft buff colour.

Available Summer to early autumn in gardens.
Cutting and preparation Easy to please. Pick straight into water. Often preserves itself in an arrangement, or can be dried by hanging.
Remarks Found in every keen arranger's garden, where it seeds very readily. Blends well with most colours.

Allium
Decorative onion
Bulb

Colour Greenish-brown flowerheads in *A. siculum*, lilac-purple in *A. rosenbachianum*. You may also find pink and yellow alliums.
Available Spring to summer in gardens. Seedheads can be dried for winter use.
Cutting and preparation Never arrange into hot water, as this brings out the scent of onions. When drying seedheads, hang each one separately to preserve the rounded shape.
Remarks Larger seedheads are ideal for winter decorations when spray-painted or spangled with glitter.

Angelica archangelica
Holy ghost
Culinary herb

Colour Soft green flowerheads, soft green or brown seedheads. Foliage yellows as it fades.
Available Summer and autumn in gardens. Seedheads can be dried for winter.
Cutting and preparation Best picked when mature, as seedhead is forming. Condition by putting stem ends in boiling water. Likes deep water in containers. Dry by hanging.
Remarks Excellent for large designs, especially pedestals. As an annual, it dies after flowering, so leave a head behind to seed.

1 *Acacia armata* **2** *Helipterum albicans* (see *Acroclinium*) **3** *Angelica archangelica* **4** *Alchemilla mollis* **5** *Allium rosenbachianum*

Antirrhinum
Snapdragon
Usually grown as an annual

Colour White, yellow, orange, red or pink flowers.
Available Spring and summer in the garden and occasionally from florists in summer.
Cutting and preparation Hammer or slice the stem ends. Allow a long, deep drink before arranging.

Ballota pseudodictamnus
Perennial

Colour Soft grey-green woolly leaves and bracts. Tiny purple flowers.
Available Foliage all the year, bracts and flowers in summer from the garden.
Cutting and preparation Put stem ends in boiling water for a few minutes. Leaves and flowers are best removed to show off the charming bracts.

Bergenia
Elephants' ears
Hardy perennial

Colour Green foliage, in some varieties colouring to plum in winter. Pink or white flowers.
Available Foliage can be used all year round, flowers in the spring, from the garden.
Cutting and preparation Give a deep pre-arrangement drink in lukewarm water.
Remarks Handsome drumstick flowers and sturdy leaves last for ages in arrangements.

Calystegia
Convolvulus or Bindweed
Perennial weed

Colour White and rose flowers, or pink with white stripes.
Available June to August in hedges or in the garden.
Cutting and preparation Cut individual flowers or pick short sprays of buds and flowers. Buds will open in water.

Arrange at once in warm water.
Remarks Beautiful flowers, short-lived but prolific. It is nice to get your own back on a weed!

Chrysanthemum
Annual or perennial

Colour White, yellow, flame, gentle red, pink, etc.
Available Summer and autumn in gardens, but now commercially available for most of the year.
Cutting and preparation Break rather than cut the stems to the right length, then hammer stem ends. A pre-arrangement drink in deep water will make them last longer.
Remarks A great stand-by for winter decorations. Florists' spray chrysanthemums may be cut down into many shorter stems. Mop-headed, double petalled chrysanthemums are not so easy to use as the spray and single daisy-flowered types but are most useful as the dominant flowers in a large pedestal or for modern styles of arrangement. Annual chrysanthemums grown from seed are enchanting.

Clarkia
Annual

Colour White, pink and purple flowers in a wide variety of tones.
Available Summer in the garden, but easily preserved for winter posies; occasionally available in florists.
Cutting and preparation Pick when almost all the flowers are open, or the stem tips will tend to keel over. Give a pre-arrangement drink in shallow hot water.
Remarks To preserve, take off any foliage and arrange the flowers in shallow water. They will then dry off in the arrangement.

1 *Clarkia pulchella* **2** *Ballota pseudodictamnus* **3** Spider-flowered White Spider chrysanthemum **4** *Convolvulus arvensis* (see *Calystegia*) **5** Dwarf bedding antirrhinum **6** *Bergenia purpurascens* Ballawley

Clematis vitalba
Traveller's joy and Old man's beard
Wild deciduous climber

Colour Green-white flowers, green seedheads changing to soft smoky grey.
Available July to September in the wild, found in hedges, usually on chalky soil.
Cutting and preparation Hammer the stem ends, give hot water drink. Preserve by glycerine method at green fruiting stage or as sprays of foliage before flowers open. Late in season remove leaves and spray the mature feathery fruits with hair lacquer to prevent disintegration.
Remarks Ideal for outline material in pedestals and other large designs.

Clivia
Kaffir lily
Bulb flower and greenhouse perennial

Colour Clear, lighthearted clusters of orange flowers; green strappy leaves.
Available Spring and summer grown as a houseplant or bought as cut flowers from florists.
Cutting and preparation No fuss — just cut and arrange, but the flowers need plenty of water.
Remarks Use the whole glorious flowerhead on its sturdy stem in large designs, but use individual flowers in small decorations.

Cobaea scandens
Cup and saucer vine
Greenhouse or half-hardy climber, usually grown as annual

Colour Subtle greenish-violet bells set in a pretty green cup.
Available Flowers July to October in the greenhouse or garden, seedheads autumn.

Cutting and preparation Cut straight into warm water.
Remarks Flowers will preserve in desiccant for temporary decoration.

Dahlia
Half-hardy perennial tuber

Colour Wide range — almost every colour except blue.
Available Summer and autumn in gardens, and sometimes in florists.
Cutting and preparation Dahlias bloom well and can be picked almost daily. Give a boiling water drink when picked, then an overnight drink. Add a couple of teaspoonsful of sugar to the arrangement water.
Remarks Individual flowers can be preserved by the desiccant method.

Delphinium
Hardy perennial

Colour White, pink, cream and many shades of blue and mauve.
Available Summer from gardens and florists. Will dry for winter.
Cutting and preparation Fill hollow stems with water and plug with cotton wool. Flowers need a good long drink before arranging. Preserve by hanging when buds are almost all open.
Remarks Useful pointed shapes for large decorations. Side sprays and individual flowers can be used in smaller designs. Preserve individual flowers in a desiccant for pot-pourri, pictures and decorations.

Dianthus caryophyllus
Carnation
Perennial

Colour Almost every colour except blue in the many varieties; however sometimes dyed blue by florists.
Available Summer in the

1 The seedhead of *Clematis vitalba* **2** *Delphinium* hybrid **3** *Dahlia* Gerrie Hoek **4** *Dianthus carophyllus* **5** *Cobaea scandens* **6** *Clivia x cyrtanthiflora*

garden and greenhouse, but through the year in florists.
Cutting and preparation Cut with a slanting cut between the nodes (the hard lumps along the stems from which the leaves spring) or the flower will not drink. Arrange into warm water.
Remarks Florist's carnations often come with small side shoots which can be pulled off and rooted in a pot. The spray varieties of carnations, with many flowers to a stem, are an excellent buy and will cut down to make a number of individual stems. Carnations will preserve instantly if the whole flower is sprayed all over with car body paint from an aerosol can; give each carnation three light coats and leave to dry.

Dicentra
Bleeding heart, Lady-in-the-bath
Perennial

Colour White or pink flowers, pretty green fern-like leaves.
Available Spring and summer from gardens.

Cutting and preparation Shallow hot water drink, then a deep, cool long drink.
Remarks Foliage of *D. formosa* is invaluable for cutting over a long period, being specially delightful in autumn, when it often colours superbly. *D. spectabilis* is useful in quite large pedestal designs after good pre-arrangement care. It can be forced into early flower by bringing roots indoors in a big pot in February.

Digitalis
Foxglove
Biennial

Colour Cultivated kinds these days are a far cry from the woodland pink-purple. Varieties now available with parchment, gold, sulphur, crushed strawberry, or bright pink flowers as well as white. Most still have appealing freckles inside the bell.
Available Flowers in summer, seedheads in autumn and winter, from flowers growing wild in British woods and country roadsides, or cultivated

in gardens.
Cutting and preparation Gather when half the flowers are fully out. Crush stem ends. Give hot water drink then an overnight deep drink.
Remarks Excellent pointed shapes for outlines in large arrangements up to pedestal size, and a joy when arranged alone on a pinholder in a shallow container.

Elaeagnus
Silver berry
Evergreen and deciduous shrubs

Colour White flowers. *E. pungens aureo variegata* has foliage of green and gold. *E. ebbingei* has green leaves with silver-grey undersides. Delightful silver-grey fruits in spring.
Available Foliage almost all the year round in gardens; sweet-scented flowers in late October.
Cutting and preparation Hammer ends of stems. Foliage and fruits will preserve by glycerine method.
Remarks E. ebbingei is

invaluable to a flower arranger. Arrange the leaves, wrong way up, with white, pink, red or yellow flowers and you will see why! Effective in both large and small arrangements. *Elaeagnus* is extremely long-lasting when cut.

Erica
Heather
Evergreen shrubby plant

Colour White, pink or lavender flowers, some with green, gold, grey, tan or warm apricot foliage.
Available Something showing every month — foliage all the year round and flowers in spring, summer, autumn or winter, according to variety, from gardens and heathland.
Cutting and preparation Flowers can often be arranged without water to prevent mildewing of stems. Dry large sprays by hanging method; small sprigs can be pressed for dried flower pictures. Newly-opened blooms keep the best colour. Many if left preserve themselves in an arrangement.

1 *Digitalis purpurea* Excelsior
2 *Dicentra spectabilis*
3 *Erica arborea alpina*
4 *Elaeagnus ebbingei* coming in to flower

1 *Escallonia x rigida* Peach Blossom 2 *Eucalyptus gunii* showing juvenile foliage 3 Ferns in a garden setting 4 *Forsythia suspensa atrocaulis* with young purple stems

Escallonia
Shrub

Colour Arching sprays of green leaves and pretty rose-red or white flowers.
Available Flowers in summer, foliage over a long period in gardens, especially near the sea.
Cutting and preparation Pound stems and give boiling water drink, then deep cool drink.
Remarks Light pointed material for outlining both large and small designs.

Eucalyptus gunnii
Australian gumtree
Shrub or tree

Colour Grey-green leaves with a strong blue tinge. Greenish-white flowers.
Available Foliage all year round from gardens and florists.
Cutting and preparation The beautiful grey-blue very juvenile leaves can be difficult to condition; a boiling water pre-arrangement drink is helpful. Short sprays will preserve in dessicant. As leaves mature they become far less tricky and no pre-arrangement care is required. They can be preserved by the glycerine method when they take on a reddish colour.
Remarks Plants can be made to grow juvenile leaves, which are round (older leaves are sickle-shaped), if the whole plant is cut down to near ground level every spring. A mature tree produces bark which peels away naturally; the longer pieces when dried create remarkably interesting shapes and colours for dried flower collages, naturalistic landscape designs and modern abstract work. Leaves and flowers often dry off in an arrangement and my own experience has proved that they will last attractively for many years.

Ferns
Many varieties with different characteristics

Colour Mostly green-leaved. Some start brown and furry as they unfurl. Used 'wrong side up' they show their attractive, brown, fruiting spore patterns.
Available All the year round from indoor pot plants. Some hardy outdoor varieties are evergreen. Otherwise available from spring to autumn in the garden or in the wild. Can be preserved for winter use.
Cutting and preparation All ferns should be cut straight into water, then left to float or submerge overnight in water.
Remarks The unfurling croziers of some ferns make a pleasing decoration if cut to different stem heights and arranged on a pinholder. Preserve fronds for winter use by pressing immediately they are gathered. Alternatively they can be treated by the glycerine method. Preserved ferns can be decorated with glitter and paint for Christmas decorations.

Forsythia
Golden bells
Deciduous shrub

Colour Various tints and shades of yellow flowers.
Available Early spring in gardens and occasionally from florists.
Cutting and preparation Hammer stems and give a hot drink.
Remarks Forsythia can be forced into early flower over a period of about five weeks.

Freesia
Corms

Colour A variety of shades, both vivid and pastel, each as lovely as its scent, set off by mid-green, lanceolate leaves.

1 *Freesia x kewensis* 2 *Geranium himalayense* 3 Ornamental grass — *Miscanthus sinensis Zebrinus* 4 *Gypsophila paniculata* Bristol Fairy 5 *Hedera helix* Goldheart

Available Most of the year from florists. From February in a cool greenhouse, and July to September in the garden from treated corms.

Cutting and preparation Cut when the lower blooms open and remove them as they die. If you need to travel with a bunch of freesias, wrap the stem ends in damp cotton wool kept in place with a rubber band.

Remarks Watch out for the lovely double kinds — these last a very long time.

Geranium
Crane's bill
Hardy perennial (see also *Pelargonium*)

Colour Blue, white, pink, or purple flowers. Foliage normally green but often colours in autumn.

Available Late spring, summer, autumn, depending on variety, from gardens; some varieties found in the wild.

Cutting and preparation A drink in shallow boiling water, followed by a deep long cool drink.

Remarks Foliage is particularly useful. The blooms are very attractive but not often seen as cut flowers. Seedheads are suitable material in miniature arrangements.

Grasses
Various ornamental kinds

Colour Flowering heads provide a range of smudgy colours, including green, brown and olive.

Available Summer and early autumn from gardens, hedgerows and wasteland. Imported varieties from florists and flower clubs.

Cutting and preparation Gather before the grass starts to seed. Arrange at once or hang to dry in small bunches.

Remarks Use fresh or dried grasses, to create slim airy shapes in mixed arrangements. They are invaluable in simple, cottagey designs but use stems in groups to avoid a fussy effect.

Gypsophila
Chalk plant or Baby's breath
Annuals and perennials

Colour White or soft pink flowers.

Available June to August from gardens and florists; preserve for winter.

Cutting and preparation Give hot water drink. Dry perfect sprays of fully-open flowers by hanging.

Remarks Very pretty flowers which are coming back into favour with arrangers. Lovely for weddings and summer party decorations. When dried, useful in swags and pressed flower pictures.

Hedera
Ivy
Climbing evergreens

Colour Green foliage, sometimes marbled with white or yellow, or splashed with cream or bronze. Leaves in a variety of sizes and shapes, according to species. Many gain a pink tinge in frosty weather. Greenish-yellow flowers and emerald green or black fruits, in some varieties.

Available Foliage all year round, berries in winter from plants in gardens and in the wild. Ivies also grow well in containers, as houseplants.

Cutting and preparation Hammer stems, give boiling water drink followed by deep, cool overnight drink.

Remarks The long-lived foliage is useful individually or in trailing sprays. Both foliage and berries preserve well by glycerine treatment.

Helichrysum
Everlasting flowers
Annual

Colour White, yellow, pink and dark wine red flowers.
Available Summer and autumn from gardens, shops, and flower club sales tables; preserve for winter use.
Cutting and preparation Harvest at all stages, except when the centres of the flowers are showing. Take only the flowerheads, not the stems, and make artificial stems from florist's wire, or dry whole flower with stem by hanging upside down.
Remarks Old favourites for winter decorations.

Helleborus
Christmas rose, Lent rose, or Hellebore
Hardy perennial

Colour White, green, soft purple or plum-coloured flowers, often endearingly freckled inside. Green foliage.
Available Flowers in winter and early spring; foliage useful for much of the year: from gardens.
Cutting and preparation A notoriously difficult cut flower when young. Take flowerheads only and float them in low bowls as an arrangement. For use in larger decorations, split the stems right up one side to open them up. Give a shallow hot water drink and then a deep warm overnight drink. Individual flowers will preserve easily in desiccant.
Remarks To protect the early flowers in the garden, cover with a cloche.

Hosta
Funkia or Plantain lily
Hardy perennial

Colour Ornamental foliage is bluish-grey, green, or green with cream or yellow. White or lavender flowers, green seedheads that turn brown.
Available Foliage, spring, summer and autumn; preserve for winter. Flowers, mainly summer. From gardens.
Cutting and preparation Give a long deep drink or submerge leaves in cool water. Flagging leaves will revive with shallow hot water drink. Leaves will slowly dry into curling brown shapes if left for a few weeks in water in an arrangement. Foliage can be pressed, seedheads dried by hanging.
Remarks One of the most popular flower arranger's plants. The foliage is useful for all kinds of designs.

Hydrangea
Deciduous
Shrub

Colour Green, cream, slate, baby blue, delicate pink or rich red flowerheads.
Available Summer and autumn from gardens, greenhouses and florists. Dry flowerheads for winter use.
Cutting and preparation Don't gather until they feel firm and really mature. Remove all foliage, hammer stems, and give boiling water treatment, then immerse flowerheads and stems in cool water for an hour. Arrange, and spray once or twice a day if flowerheads are immature. Individual flowers of all ages can be pressed. Harvest heads for preserving at the end of summer and dry off in a little water.

Iris
Sword flower
Perennial

Colour A wide range of colours in the flowers. *Iris foetidissima* (Gladwyn Iris) is grown for its wonderful orange seeds. Mostly green foliage, but some varieties have variegated leaves.
Available May to July, depending on variety, in gardens. The water iris grows wild. Commercially grown flowers available from florists almost all the year round.
Cutting and preparation Pick in bud. Remove any white part at the bottom of the stem with a slanting cut. A light spray of clear varnish or lacquer will hold the bright seed of *Iris foetidissima* for many months.

1 *Helichrysum bracteatum*
2 *Helleborus niger macrophylla*
3 *Hosta ventricosa* Variegata
4 *Hydrangea macrophylla macrophylla*
5 Fruit of *Iris foetidissima*

Jasminum
Winter, Spring and Summer
Jasmine
Tender and hardy shrubs or
climbing plants

Colour Yellow or white flowers.
Available J. nudiflorum is the
popular hardy winter jasmine,
flowering from November to
February. *J. primulinum*
(tender) flowers in March and
April, *J. officinale* (hardy), June
to September, *J. polyanthum*
(tender, often sold as a house
plant), winter and early spring.
Grown in gardens and as
houseplants.
Cutting and preparation Pick
sprays of winter jasmine in bud
and bring indoors to open.
Other kinds appreciate a deep
drink before arranging.
Remarks Every arranger should
grow winter jasmine. It
flourishes best against a
sheltered wall.

Lathyrus odoratus
Sweet pea
Annual

Colour All colours.
Available June to September
from gardens and florists.
Cutting and preparation Cut
with the longest stems possible
when the first flowers open.
Give a deep drink.
Remarks Particularly charming
when arranged simply on their
own. The old-fashioned
varieties listed in seed
catalogues have outstanding
fragrance but smaller blooms
than the more common kinds.
For the tiniest gardens there
are types which grow no higher
than nine inches but bloom
prolifically.

Lilium
Lily
Bulb

Colour Ivory, cream, gold, pink,
bronze or orange flowers, some
spotted and some with a
different colour on the backs of
the petals.
Available Over many months,
depending on variety in
gardens. All the year from
florists.
Cutting and preparation
Hammer woody stems, then
give deep drink in cool water.
Pick stems when the first
flowers are opening. Leave
some foliage behind to feed the
bulb. Good seedheads will dry
by hanging.
Remarks Ideal for church
decoration, weddings, exotic
parties — lilies are always eye-
catching, but the perfume can
be overpowering in a small
room.

Lunaria
Honesty
Biennial

Colour Velvety purple,
lavender-rose, and sometimes
white flowers. Green seedheads
stained with plum, turn buff
when dried and finally
transparent and silvery when
the outer husk is removed.
There is a superb variegated
form with leaves the colour of
mint and cream.
Available Flowers, May and
June. Seedheads, summer,
autumn, and dried for winter.
From gardens and florists.
Cutting and preparation
Flowers need a hot water drink,
soak stems overnight. Gather
some seedheads fresh and
arrange green. Allow others to
'go to seed' and gently rub
away the outer membrane to
expose the inner secret 'moons'
for use in winter arrangements.
Seedheads will preserve by
glycerine method if picked
when green.
Remarks The dried 'moons' can
be spray-painted in pastel
colours as a delicate contrast to
the natural silvery tone.

1 *Jasminum nudiflorum* **2** *Lathyrus odoratus* **3** *Lilium speciosum*
hybrid **4** *Lunaria annua* (immature seed pods)

Matthiola
Ten-week or Brompton stock
Annual or hardy biennial

Colour Soft yellow, pale pink, crimson, pale or deep mauve flowers.
Available The ten-week variety is sown in March, gathered in June. Brompton Stock is sown in June to give flowers the following summer. From gardens and florists.
Cutting and preparation Remove all leaves which might go below water level in the arrangement. Hammer hard stem ends and give boiling water drink followed by long, cool deep drink.
Remarks Invaluable flowers for the arranger and the pleasant scent is a bonus.

Muscari
Grape hyacinth
Bulb

Colour White and various shades of blue flowers. Green seedheads turn buff.
Available Spring, seedheads summer; from gardens and florists.
Cutting and preparation No special treatment required. Seedheads dry on the plant.
Remarks Their attractive scent makes them particularly good flowers to use for bedroom arrangements.

Narcissus
Daffodil
Bulb

Colour White, yellow, orange or soft pink flowers.
Available In gardens, February to May. From the shops, mid-winter to late spring. Rarely in the wild, where they should never be picked.
Cutting and preparation Pick or buy in bud, showing the petal colour. Best arranged in water rather than flower foams. Re-

cut any split stems to make arranging easier. Like most bulb flowers, they live longest in shallow-water dish-type arrangements.
Remarks Grow daffodils in wide variety in the garden in sizes ranging from tiny 7.5cm (3 in) stem varieties to the large double-petalled.

Orchidaceae
Orchid
Perennial

Colour Cream to green, soft pink, rose, lavender or purple flowers.
Available All the year round from greenhouses and florists.
Cutting and preparation Cut with a slanting cut and stand in deep water. Re-cut the stem end of shop-bought blooms.
Remarks One of the longest-lasting cut flowers.

Papaver
Poppy
Annuals and hardy perennials

Colour Yellow, white, pink, apricot and brilliant scarlet flowers. Green seedheads turn soft brown. Green foliage.
Available Foliage of perennial kinds can be cut from March. Flowers, late spring and summer. Seedheads, summer and autumn; preserve for winter. From gardens, roadside verges and wasteland. Large imported seedheads from florists and flower clubs.
Cutting and preparation Burn or boil stem ends and give long pre-arrangement drink. Pick flowers when buds are just bursting. Dry seedheads by hanging.
Remarks Perennial poppies' seedheads sometimes skeletonise naturally on the plant in late autumn, appearing like tiny birdcages, which can be sprayed with glitter or metallic paint.

1 *Matthiola* Brompton stock
2 *Paphiopedilum* — the slipper orchid 3 *Muscari armeniacum* Blue Spike, a species of grape hyacinth 4 *Narcissus* Texas
5 *Papaver rhoeas* The Shirley

Pelargonium
Bedding and Greenhouse
geranium
Perennial

Colour White, pink, red or
orange flowers. Many superb
colourings in the foliage of
different varieties.
Available Foliage all year
round. Flowers, late spring,
summer and autumn. From
houseplants, gardens,
greenhouses and florists.
Cutting and preparation Handle
the flowers by the stalks, as
they are easily damaged.
Gather when first flowers are
opening and there are many
buds still to emerge. Cut stems
from plant and remove any
hard lower portion.
Remarks Unusual material for
both massed arrangements and
more austere modern designs
and could more often be seen
as a cut flower. The foliage is
always useful.

Petunia
Annual

Colour Charming soft pinks,
lavender-blues, white, purples,
and jolly reds.
Available Summer in gardens,
though a large tub of market-
bought plants brought into a
porch or cold greenhouse in
May can give flowers non-stop
until October.
Cutting and preparation Gather
the longest stems the plant can
spare. Give hot water drink
followed by deep, cool
overnight drink.
Remarks The wide range of
colours makes this a favourite
flower for cutting.

Phaseolus coccineus
Runner bean
Grown as an annual

Colour White flowers in some
varieties, pink or orange-red in
others. Green or purple pods.

Available Summer and autumn
from vegetable gardens.
Cutting and preparation Cut
when the first flowers open.
Pick beans with a little stem to
make arranging easier. Arrange
immediately after picking.
Remarks Both flowers and pods
bring distinction to summer
designs of flowers, fruits and
vegetables. Bean crops are
usually so good that a row will
easily spare a few flowers and
pods for arrangement.

Philadelphus
Mock orange
Shrub

Colour Creamy-white flowers.
There is a golden-leaved form
as opposed to the usual green.
Available Flowers, June and
July. Foliage, late spring,
summer, autumn. From
gardens.
Cutting and preparation
Remove almost all leaves.
Hammer stems, then give
boiling water treatment and a
deep, cool drink. Hard to revive
if the flowers flag, so pick
straight into water.
Remarks A delight for
weddings when arranged with
other white or pastel flowers.

Physalis
Chinese or Japanese lantern
Hardy perennial

Colour Green seed vessels,
turning to the familiar orange.
Available Summer and autumn
from gardens, florists and
markets. Preserve for winter.
Cutting and preparation Gather
some seedheads green, others
fully coloured. Remove all
leaves and dry by hanging in a
bunch.
Remarks Pleasing for Christmas
when lightly gilded, or can be
gently cut open to make a
flower shape which shows off
the orange seedpod within.

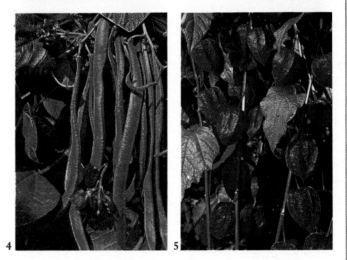

1 *Pelargonium x domesticum* Carisbrooke 2 *Petunia x hybrida*
Summer Sun 3 *Philadelphus x virginalis* Virginal 4 *Phaseolus
coccineus* Streamline (runner bean) 5 *Physalis alkekengi* (Chinese
lantern)

Quercus
Oak
Tree

Colour Green or brown fruits (acorns).
Available Summer and autumn in the wild or gardens. Catkins of male oak in spring.
Cutting and preparation Branches with catkins should be hammered at the end and given a hot water drink.
Remarks A well-shaped branch with catkins is attractive in a shallow dish surrounded by daffodils, for example. Pick acorns from the tree, rather than those already fallen. Acorns are useful for winter decoration and swags. If fruits come out of their 'cups' they can easily be glued back in again.

Ribes
Flowering currant
Shrub

Colour Red, pink, greenish-yellow or white flowers. Attractive green foliage.
Available Flowers, spring. Foliage, spring, summer, autumn. From gardens.
Cutting and preparation Hammer stems. Give hot water drink then deep, cool drink. Can be brought into early bloom by bringing branches into the house in January.
Remarks The redcurrant and blackcurrant also belong to this family and give flowers as well as the pretty fruits.

Rheum
Rhubarb
Hardy perennial

Colour There are ornamental varieties that have coloured leaves in spring, but ordinary rhubarb forced into early leaf has striking lime-yellow foliage and red-pink stems and is every bit as pleasing.
Available Late winter and spring, from gardens and greengrocers.
Cutting and preparation Arrange forced rhubarb at once. Cut stems to different lengths, or use leaves only and cook the rest!
Remarks Lovely when arranged on a pinholder in a shallow container, perhaps with tulips or daffodils. the coloured leaves greatly add to the impact of mixed spring arrangements.

Rosa
Rose
Perennial shrub

Colour Just about everything but blue in the flowers. Green, orange, red and black fruit (hips). Some roses have large decorative thorns.
Available Flowers, summer and autumn. Hips, autumn and winter. Florists have roses the year round. From gardens, shops, and in the wild.
Cutting and preparation Pick short sprays of wild roses in close-to-opening bud. Remove at least the lower thorns of all roses. Hammer stem ends, and give hot water and deep pre-arrangement drinks. Revive flagging blooms by re-cutting stems and treating with boiling water. Rose foliage can be preserved by the glycerine method. Double scarlet roses in late summer will usually preserve if left out of water on top of a radiator.
Remarks The old-fashioned shrub roses give a period flavour to any arrangement.

Scabiosa
Scabious
Annuals and hardy perennials

Colour Lavender-blue, white, yellow or crimson flowers.
Scabiosa stellata Drumstick, a hardy annual, has powder-blue flowers and bronze seedheads.

1 Acorns of *Quercus cerris* 2 *Ribes laurifolium* 3 *Rosa rugosa* Frau Dagmar Hastrup 4 *Rheum alexandrae* 5 *Scabiosa caucasia* Clive Greaves

Available Early to late summer. Seedheads of *S. stellata* in autumn for preservation. From gardens, and occasionally flowers from florists.

Cutting and preparation Give a long drink in cold water before arranging. Buds will open in water, but to a paler colour than flowers opened while still growing. preserve seedheads by hanging.

Remarks *S. stellata* Drumstick's enchanting seedheads are marvellous for winter use in small arrange-ments when preserved and for pressed flower decorations.

Syringa
Lilac
Shrub

Colour Purple, pink, or white flowers. Brown seedheads.

Available May and June in gardens, also stocked by florists in winter and spring.

Cutting and preparation Longer stems seem to last better than short. Pick straight into water removing all foliage

immediately. Hammer stem ends; give boiling water drink and a deep, cool overnight drink.

Remarks Cut separate branches of lilac foliage to arrange with the flowers, but keep flowering branches stripped of leaves.

Tulipa
Tulip
Bulb

Colour Flowers in a wide range of colours — white, green, yellow, apricot to orange, pink to red, lavender to purple. Some varieties have flowers streaked and feathered with other colours.

Available Winter and spring from greenhouses and florists; spring only from gardens.

Cutting and preparation Cut off any hard white parts at the ends of the stems. To straighten curved stems, roll in newspaper and leave in a deep drink for a few hours. Prick very early forced tulips just below the flowerheads with a pin, to help them take up

water. Some people add sugar to the arrangement water.

Remarks Because of their tendency to bend their stems in an arrangement, so that the design changes shape, tulips are not really suitable for competitive flower arrangement.

Viburnum tinus and V. opulus
Laurustinus and Gelder rose
Shrub

Colour Green to white flowers, growing in clusters.

Available *V. tinus* has winter flowers and all-year-round foliage, with bright blue berries in summer. *V. opulus* flowers in June but is available as a florists' flower in spring and summer. Found in gardens, markets and florists.

Cutting and preparation *V. tinus* is an easy cut flower, *V. opulus* more difficult to work with. Remove most of the leaves of *V. opulus*, hammer the stem ends, and give boiling water drink followed by a long, cool

overnight drink.

Remarks The luxurious 'snowballs' of *V. opulus* are lime-green at first then turn white; a luxurious addition to large flowerpieces. *V. tinus* is perfection for homely posies, and has evergreen leaves.

Zantedeschia aethiopica
Arum lily
Rhizome

Colour White flowers, with bold yellow 'tongue', heart-shaped green leaves. There is a green-flowered form.

Available Spring, from greenhouses, gardens and florists.

Cutting and preparation Give long drink, immersing stems right up to the flowerheads. Leaves stiffen if floated in starch water overnight.

Remarks Flower and leaf stems, if appearing too formal, may be gently curved by smoothing and stroking between the fingers. Superb flowers for all stately effects and important occasions.

1 *Syringa x prestoniae* **2** *Tulipa* Purissima **3** *Zantedeschia aethiopica* **4** *Viburnum opulus* Compactum, in winter, bearing its translucent red fruit.

You may have read this book for purely practical reasons, and then discovered that arranging flowers gives you much pleasure and that you seem to have a natural aptitude for it which you wish to develop. You can put your name down on your church or chapel flower rota, take a course at day or evening classes and join a flower arrangement club. Inquire first at your public library for details of local clubs. Information can also be obtained from the National Association of Flower Arrangement Societies of Great Britain (NAFAS). NAFAS is the national authority responsible for training and authorizing judges and demonstrators.

Day and evening classes in flower arranging are organized by many Further Education centres and Evening Institutes. Again, you can find details of classes held near your home from the library or your local education office. The City and Guilds of London Institute organizes courses and examinations and will' supply details of what is available.

There are flower arrangement clubs and societies in many parts of the world. Ikebana International, a Japanese-based society, has groups in Britain and other countries, for example. The World Association of Flower Arrangers can supply information about clubs and groups in many countries if you want to take a wider interest. You may also find you need more specialised information about the plant material you use and there are a number of national groups dedicated to particular plants or categories of horticulture that may be able to provide practical advice.

Useful addresses

National Association of Flower Arrangement Societies of Great Britain (NAFAS), 21a Denbigh Street, London SW1.

City and Guilds of London Institute, 46 Britannia Street, London WC1.

World Association of Flower Arrangers, 21a Denbigh Street, London SW1.

Ikebana International, CPO Box 1262, Tokyo, Japan.

The Royal Horticultural Society, Vincent Square, London SW1.

The Royal National Rose Society, Chiswell Green Lane, St Albans, Herts.

The British National Carnation Society, 3 Canberra Close, Hornchurch, Essex. Secretary, Mrs P.E. Diamond.

The Daffodil Society, 1 Dorset Cottages, Birch Road, Copford, Colchester, Essex. Secretary, Mr D.J. Pearce.

The National Dahlia Society, 26 Burns Road, Lillington, Leamington Spa, Warwickshire. Secretary, Mr P. Damp.

The Delphinium Society, 11 Long Grove, Seer Green, Bucks. Secretary, Mr C.R. Edwards.

The National Chrysanthemum Society, 65 St Margaret's Avenue, Whetstone, London N20. Secretary, Mrs S.G. Gosling.

The British Gladiolus Society, 10 Sandbach Road, Thurlwood, Rode Heath, Stoke-on-Trent, Staffs. Secretary, Mrs M. Rowley.

The British Iris Society, 67 Bushwood Road, Kew, Surrey. Secretary, Mr G.E. Cassidy.

The National Sweet Pea Society, Acacia Cottage, Ampney, near Cirencester, Glos. Secretary, Mr L.H.O. Williams.

Suppliers of non-plant materials
Many firms specialize in supplying non-plant materials for flower arranging; such as containers, bases, driftwood, pinholders, pedestals and mechanics. These are retailed through florists, garden centres, large department stores and flower-arranging clubs. Names and addresses of wholesale suppliers can be found in their advertisements in 'The Flower Arranger'.

Publications
'The Flower Arranger' is the official magazine of NAFAS. Obtainable through flower arrangement clubs or from Taylor Bloxham Ltd., Nugent Street, Leicester.

Gardens to visit
Unusual and interesting plants and shrubs can be seen in the gardens of many stately homes and private houses which are open to the public from time to time. Details from:
The National Trust, 42 Queen Anne's Gate, London SW1.
The National Gardens Scheme, 57 Lower Belgrave Square, London SW1.

Adhesive clay A synthetic clay-like substance, such as Plasticine. Pressed into the base of a container, it keeps pinholders and other supports firmly in place. Easily moulded into shape, and reusable.

Air-drying A way of preserving flowers and grasses. The plant material is hung upside-down or stored upright in containers in a dry, warm atmosphere, and protected from strong light.

Annual A plant which completes its life-cycle – from the sowing of seed through growth, flowering or producing fruit – within a year, and then dies.

Artist's fixative A lacquer-like substance which can be sprayed onto dried flowers to make them less fragile and improve their appearance.

Atomizer A device which sprays water in a fine mist. Useful for refreshing arrangements.

Balance The correct proportions and distribution of plant material in an arrangement which produces a stable and pleasing effect.

Biennial A plant which produces flowers or fruit the year after sowing seed.

Bract Leaf-like parts of a plant, protecting undeveloped shoots or buds. Sometimes bracts are highly coloured, as in the case of poinsettias.

Calyx A ring of leaves enclosing an unopened bud.

Candlecups Shallow 'cups' with a plug on the underside which fits into the neck of a bottle or a candlestick.

Cereals Grasses such as barley, oats and wheat. They can be preserved by drying, and used for decorative purposes.

Conditioning The treatment of plant material before it is arranged, in order to prolong its life and retain its best appearance.

Deciduous A tree or shrub which annually sheds its leaves at the end of the growing season.

Desiccants Substances used in the desiccating process for absorbing moisture.

Desiccation A process for preserving flowers by drawing out their moisture. The flowers are placed in an airtight container with a desiccant.

Driftwood A piece of wood which has been dried or weathered by the elements. It can be used as a base for an arrangement or to conceal pinholders or mechanics, or purely to add interest and texture to a display.

Fillers Plant material that contrasts with the eye-catching areas in an arrangement, adding to their effect without distracting attention from them.

Florist's tape see *Gutta percha.*

Foam blocks Shaped in bricks or cylinders, these are made from a synthetic foam substance into which stems can be pressed and supported. There are two types: one is used dry for dried flower displays; the other, for use with fresh flowers, is soaked before using and then kept moist. Available from florists, foam blocks can be cut to fit containers of all shapes.

Focal point The central point of an arrangement to which the eye is naturally drawn, and the main area of interest in the display.

Foliage The leaves of plants or trees. In show work, this can also include bracts and unopened buds which do not show petal colour.

Glycerine A liquid which can be used to preserve leaves, berries and some flowers, keeping them supple and altering their colours in the process.

Gutta percha or florist's binding tape. An adhesive tape, available in green, white or brown, which is used to conceal wire stems.

Hardy plants Those plants which are capable of withstanding low temperatures.

Holding material see *Mechanics.*

Ikebana The Japanese art of arranging flowers, following a code of symbolic meanings and strict rules.

Jardinière An ornamental pot or stand for holding indoor plants.

Mechanics The equipment, such as pinholders, foam blocks and wire netting, used for holding plant material in arrangements. Concealed inside containers or by foliage, the mechanics allow for an almost unlimited scope in flower display.

Modelling compound see *Adhesive clay.*

Niche A shallow recess, usually in a wall. In show work, this refers to a backing with side pieces.

Nosegay A small, traditional bunch which includes some scented flowers and which, in the past, was often carried or worn.

Perennial A plant which continues to produce flowers or fruit year after year.

Pinholder A series of pins projecting from a heavy, metal base. Fixed into a container, the pins hold stems in position.

Pot-pourri A mixture of scented dried petals.

Secateurs Clippers used with one hand for cutting plant material.

Sheaf An arrangement where flowers are laid lengthwise and tied together.

Shrub A plant whose woody stems usually grow directly from the ground, without any supporting trunk.

Skeletonizing A way of treating leaves by boiling and scrubbing to remove the soft tissue, and revealing the decorative structure of the leaf skeleton.

Stub wires Lengths of florist's wire which are used to make stems longer or more flexible, or for replacing them altogether. Also used for binding posies.

Swag A rope of flowers and foliage hung by its ends.

Water drying A process for preserving flowers by keeping the ends of the stems in water until it has been completely absorbed.

'Well' holder A version of the pinholder, with an inbuilt dish or well for holding water.

Page numbers in *Italic* refer to illustrations.

Acacia 110; *110*
Achillea 83, 86, 89; *82*
Acrolinium 110; *110*
Adhesive clay 102, 103, 104, 105
Advent ring 58; *58*
Aftercare of flower arrangements 15, 104
Air-drying method of preserving flowers and foliage 86
Alchemilla mollis 42, 48, 89, 110; *89, 110*
Alkanet 42
Allium 110; *110*
Almond, flowering 66
Alstroemeria 15, 28, 37, 83; *17, 24, 36, 72, 82*
  wiring 73
Alum 92
Amaryllis 13, 66
Ammobium 86; *87*
Anemones 66; *21*
  in baskets 30, 60; *31*
  in displays 43, 51, 79; *50, 79*
Angelica archangelica 110; *110*
Antirrhinums 32, 111; *111*
Apple blossom 15, 64, 66
Aquilegia 108
Arrangements
  and colour 16; *17*
  and design 18; *19*
  and equipment 100, 102-105
  selecting flowers for 12, 13, 32, 108, 109
  see also Special occasions
Artificial flowers 48, 54, 56, 58; *58*
Arum lilies 32, 121; *121*
Asparagus sparenduli 54
Aspidistras 32, 96; *24*
Aspirin and roses 14
Asters, China 66
Atomizers 15, 23, 51, 104
Autumn flowers 24; *24, 25*
  dried 96; *96, 97*
  see also Harvest festivals
Azaleas 66

Baby's breath *see* Gypsophila
Balance and arrangements 18, 32
Ballota 42, 111; *111*

Balsam 66
Barley 83, 86; *82*
Basil 66
Baskets 28, 88, 100, 102; *31*
  and displays 30, 83, 89; *82*
  as gifts 64, 74, 75; *75*
  Easter 60; *61*
Bay 58, 64; *95*
Beech 94, 96; *95*
Belladonna lilies 66
Bellflowers 66
Bells of Ireland 94, 96; *95, 97*
Berberis 18
Bergenia 94, 111; *111*
Berries 83, 108
  artificial 56, 58
  preserving 94; *95*
Betony 66
Binding bouquets 65, 69, 105
Bindweed 111
Bird of paradise 13
Blackberry
  fruit 94
  leaves *24, 95*
Bleaching flowers and foliage 96
Bleeding heart 113; *113*
Blossom
  forcing 15
  retarding 15
Bluebells 18, 66; *19*
Boiling water treatment 13
Borax 92
Bouquets
  dried flower 89
  florist's 10
  wedding 69, 73; *68, 72*
  wiring 73, 103; *73*
  see also Posies, Sprays
Brassica see Ornamental cabbage
Breakfast tray posies 47, 60; *46*
Bridal flowers *see* Weddings
Briza maxima see Quaking grass
Broom 66, 81; *80*
Bryony 66
Buddleia 86
Bugloss 66
Bulrushes 86
Busy Lizzie 39, 44
Buttercups 66, 92; *23*
Buying flowers 12, 13

Calceolarias 66
Californian poppy 66

Calystegia 111
Camellia
  flowers 32, 66
  leaves 43, 48; *49*
Campanulas 32, 66
Candlecups 104, 105; *105*
Candles 58; *58*
Candlesticks 102, 103, 105
Candytuft 66
Caraway 86
Carnations 12, 66, 112; *112*
  in arrangements 35, 37; *36*
  in bouquets 64, 69; *68*
  preserving 92
  spray 12, 81; *19, 80*
Celandines 66
Central heating and flowers 15
Centrepieces 42
  Christmas 58; *58*
  for buffets 42, 48; *49*
  for dinner parties 43; *43*
Cereals 28, 39, 83; *82*
  preserving 86
Chalk plant *see* Gypsophila
Cherry blossom 35, 66
Chicken wire 12, 83, 105
China aster 66
China rose 66
Chinese lanterns 119; *24, 119*
  in arrangements 56, 83, 89; *82*
  preserving 86
Chives 86
Christening parties 42, 52
Christmas decorations 42, 56, 58; *56-59*
Christmas roses 66, 116; *116*
  artificial 54
Chrysanthemums 12, 13, 64, 66, 111; *111*
  in arrangements 35, 51, 54; *34*
  spider 44, 83; *25, 111*
  spray 37, 65, 83; *24, 36*
Church decorations 78, 81; *80*
  for harvest festivals 83; *83*
  for weddings 42, 51, 52, 54, 69; *50*
Cineraria 66
Clarkia 66, 89, 111; *111*
  drying 86
Clematis 12, 66, 112; *112*
  foliage 39, 69
Clivia 112; *112*
Cobaea scandens 112; *112*
Cocktails and flowers 44

Colour 16, 28, 32; *17*
  and containers 100
  and ink 42, 48
  and special occasions 42, 48, 69
  planning schemes 69, 78, 108
Coltsfoot 66
Columbine 86; *19*
Conditioning flowers and foliage 12-14, 110-121
Cones 56, 58; *56, 57*
  wiring 88; *88*
Containers 39, 100, 102; *101*
  and hygiene 14
  and proportion 18
  and settings 28
  for drying flowers 86, 88, 92
  for special occasions 42, 47
  for transporting flowers 15
  improvising 78, 100, 102
  metal 14, 102
  narrow-necked containers 103, 104
  Oriental style 35; *34*
  weighting 48, 100
  see also Baskets, Trugs
Convulvulus 111
Coreopsis 66
Cornflowers 28, 42, 54, 64
Corsages 73
Cowslips 23, 66
Cranesbill 115; *17, 115*
Crescent-shaped arrangements 39
Cross-wiring 73; *73*
Crown imperials 32, 66
Crystallized flowers 44, 52
Cuckoo pint *19*
Cup and saucer arrangements 37, 64, 88, 102
Cupressus 54, 58, 81; *80, 95*
Currant, flowering 15, 66, 120; *120*
Cutting flowers and foliage 12, 108, 109, 110-121
Cypress 66

Daffodils 60, 66, 118; *21, 118*
Dahlias 14, 16, 66, 112; *112*
  in arrangements 42, 48, 83
Daisies 44, 66; *23, 45*
  preserving 92
Daphne 66
Day lilies 65, 66; *65*
Dehydration and remedies 15

Delphiniums 18, 112; *112*
    drying 86; *87*
Desiccation method of
    preserving flowers and
    foliage 92
Dianthus caryophyllus see
    Carnations
Dicentra 113; *113*
Digitalis see Foxgloves
Dill 86
Dinner party decorations 43;
    43
Disinfectant and *brassica* 14
Displays of flowers 78, 79; *79*
    see also Special occasions
Dog rose 66
Draughts 15
Dried flowers and foliage 39,
    56, 58; *87*
    in arrangements 88, 89, 91,
    92, 96; *90, 93, 97*
    see also Preserving flowers
Driftwood 32, 35, 104
Dyeing flowers 48, 86
    see also Gilding, Paint

Easter decorations 44, 60; *45,
    60, 61*
Egg shells 47, 60, 102
Elderflower 66
Eleagnus 113; *113*
Equipment for flower
    arranging 100, 102-105;
    101, 105
    planning 78
Erica see Heather
Escallonia 114; *114*
Eucalyptus 13, 79, 114; *114*
    and bouquets 65; *65*
    preserving 96; *95, 97*
Euphorbias 14, 42
Evergreens 54, 56, 58, 65, 70
    preserving 94
Everlasting flowers *see*
    Preserving flowers
Everlasting pearl 86; *87*

Fatsia 51
    preserving 94, 96; *94*
Fennel 86
Ferns 66, 114; *114*
    in arrangements 81; *80*
    in bouquets 64, 69
Fig 18, 94
Fireplace decorations 54, 58,
    60, 89; *59*

Floating blossoms 37, 44
Florist's foam *see* Foam blocks
Florist's tape *see* Gutta percha
Flower festivals 78
    see also Church decorations
Flowering currant 15, 66, 120;
    120
Flowers and foliage
    and food 42-44, 48, 75; *45*
    and settings 28, 32, 35; *33*
    buying 12, 13
    cutting and conditioning 12,
    13, 14, 110-121
    growing 109-121
    meanings of 64, 66-67
    selecting 108, 109
    transporting 14, 15, 64
    see also Arrangements, Gifts,
        Preserving flowers
Foam blocks 103, 104, 105
Foliage
    conditioning 13, 15
    selecting 12, 108
    see also Evergreens, Flowers
        and foliage, Leaves
Food and flowers 42-44, 48, 60;
    43, 45, 49
    and weddings 42, 52, 54; *52*
    as gifts 75; *75*
    see also Harvest festivals
Forcing flowers 15
Forget-me-nots 21, 47, 66; *21*
Forsythia 15, 114; *114*
    preserving 92
Foxgloves 28, 67, 112; *112*
    preserving 94
Freesias 70, 114-115; *114*
    in arrangements 44, 50, 52,
    81; *45, 46, 50, 52, 80*
    in bouquets 47, 69, 73; *68*
French marigolds 67
Fruit and flowers 42, 48
    and swags 42
    as gifts 75; *75*
Fuchsias 43, 67

Gaillardia 48
Garnishes 44; *45*
Geraniums 67, 115; *115*
    in arrangements 32, 56; *19*
Gerberas 56; *56*
Gifts of flowers 64, 74
    as posies 14, 15, 47, 60; *47*
    in baskets *60, 64, 75; 61, 75*
Gilding flowers and foliage 32,
    42, 56, 94; *57*

Gladioli 12, 15, 32, 42, 67
Glucose and roses 14
Glycerined foliage 24, 94; *24,
    94, 95*
Golden bells *see* Forsythia
Golden rod 86
Gorse 67
Grape hyacinths 21, 118; *21,
    118*
    in arrangements 47, 60; *20,
    46*
Grapes 48, 75
Grasses 88, 108, 115; *115*
    and displays 39, 91; *90*
    drying 86
Gratitude, flowers to express
    66, 74, 75; *74, 75*
Grevillea 13
Gutta percha
    and bouquets 69, 73
    and stems 70, 88, 103
Gypsophila 86, 70, 115; *115*
    in arrangements 51, 89; *50*
    in bouquets 47, 69; *68*
Gypsy baskets 60, 89; *61*

Hair lacquer treatment 92, 94
'Hairpin' wiring 73; *73*
Hall decorations 39
Hare's tail 86
Harvest festivals 83; *82, 83*
Hat decorations 64, 70; *70, 71*
Hawthorn 67
Hazel 15, 67
Headdresses 64, 70; *70, 71*
Heather 67, 112; *112*
    preserving 94
Hebe *21*
Hedera see Ivy
Helenium 48
Helichrysum 86, 88, 116; *87,
    116*
Heliotrope 67
Helipterum 86, 87, 89, 110;
    110
Helleborus 116; *116*
    leaves 18, 42, 75; *19, 75*
    see also Christmas roses
Hemerocallis lilies 69; *68*
Herbs 28, 44, 48
    meanings of 66-67
    preserving 86
Hibiscus 42, 67
Hogarth curve designs 18; *19*
Holding clay *see* Adhesive clay
Holding material 103-105; *105*

Holly 43, 58, 67
    preserving 96; *95*
Hollyhocks 28, 67
Holy ghost 110; *110*
Honesty 56, 57, 67, 117; *117*
Honeysuckle 14, 67
Horizontal arrangements 18;
    19
    containers for 102
Horse chestnut 15
Hosta 14, 32, 42, 116; *116*
Humid atmospheres
    flowers for 28
    remedies for 23
Hyacinths 67, 70; *21, 71*
    and displays 79, 81; *79, 80*
    preserving 92
Hydrangeas 67, 116; *116*
    in arrangements 52, 89; *29,
    52*
    preserving 86, 94

Ikebana 35; *34*
Immortelles *see* Helichrysum,
    Preserving flowers
Ink and flowers 42, 48
Irises 32, 42, 67, 116; *116*
Ivy 67, 70, 115; *115*
    and bouquets 64, 69
    and swags 42, 54, 58; *55*
    berries 56, 58
    in arrangements 30, 37, 39,
    48, 75; *31, 38*
    preserved 96; *95*

Jardinières 32
Jasmine 67, 92, 117; *117*
Jonquil 67
Juniper 54, 81; *80*

Kaffir lilies 112; *112*

Laburnum 67
Lady-in-the-bath 113; *113*
Lady's mantle *see* Alchemilla
    mollis
Lady's slipper 67
Lagurus ovatus 86
Lamium *17, 19*
Language of flowers 64, 66-67
Larkspur 54, 55, 67
    preserving 86, 92
Lathyrus odoratus see Sweet
    peas
Laurel 35, 58, 65, 67
    bleaching 96

Lavender 64, 67, 74
    scented ring 64, 74; *74*
'Lazy S' arrangements *17, 19*
Leaves 12, 32
    and posies 64, 73; *73*
    and sprays 65, 69; *65, 68*
    glycerined 24, 94; *24, 94*
    skeletonizing 94
    see also Evergreens
Light and flowers 15, 88
Lilac 12, 13, 67; *67*
Lilies 15, 67, 73, 117; *73, 117*
    and bouquets 64, 65, 69, 73; *68, 72*
    in displays 32, 51; *33, 50*
Lily-of-the-valley 47, 67, 69, 92; *46, 68*
Lime 108
Lobelia 67
London pride 67
Love-in-a-mist 55, 67
    seedheads 86, 92; *87, 93*
Love-lies-bleeding 67, 89
    drying 86
L-shaped arrangements 18, 39, 54, 81, 102; *19, 80, 91*
Lunaria see Honesty
Lupins 86

Madonna lilies 32; *33*
Magnolia 32, 35, 58, 67
Mahonia 32, 56; *21, 57*
    glycerined *24, 95*
Mallow 48, 65, 86
Marguerites 32; *19*
Marigolds 44, 48, 67, 83; *82*
Marjoram 86; *87*
Matthiola 118; *118*
Meanings of flowers 64, 66-67
Mechanics of flower arranging 103-105; *104, 105*
Metal containers 14, 102
Michaelmas daisies 67, 83
Mimosa 67, 86, 110; *110*
'Mind your own business' *see*
    Busy Lizzie
Mint 28, 44, 67
Mistletoe 67
Mock orange *see* Philadelphus
Modelling compound *see*
    Adhesive clay
Moss 13, 75
Mother's day flowers 47; *46*
Mountain ash 67
Muscari see Grape hyacinths
Myrtle 67

Narcissus 51, 67, 118; *118*
    'cheerfulness' *21*
    pheasant's eye 75; *21, 75*
Nasturtiums 44, 67
Nepita *19*
Nerines 69; *68*
Niche arrangements 18, 102

Oak 67, 120; *120*
Oats 28, 83, 86; *82*
Old man's beard *see* Clematis
Oleander 67
Olive 67
Onions 86, 110; *110*
Onopordum 32, 42
Orange blossom 67
Orchids 13, 73, 118; *118*
Oriental arrangements 35, 44; *34*
Ornamental cabbage 14, 32

Paint
    and flowers 32, 56, 94; *57*
    and containers 100, 102
Pansies 47, 67, 92; *46*
Parsley 28
Party decorations 42-44, 54, 55; *43, 55*
    see also Special occasions
Pebbles 32
Pedestal arrangements 52, 78, 104; *50, 52*
Pelargoniums 44, 119; *119*
Peonies 15, 28, 67; *19*
    tree 32
Peppermint oil 14
Periwinkles 39, 67, 69; *19*
Petunias 67, 119; *119*
Philadelphus 12, 119; *119*
Physalis see Chinese lanterns
Pillar arrangements 51, 78; *50, 51*
Pineapples 75
Pine cones 56, 58; *56, 57*
    wiring 88; *88*
Pinholders 104, 105; *105*
    concealing 32
Pinks 54, 55, 64, 67
Planning displays 78
Plants 32, 109-121
Poinsettias 14, 58
    artificial 56
Polyanthus 64, 67
Poppies 14, 28, 67, 118; *118*
    Icelandic 48; *49*
    seedpods 86

Posies
    as gifts 14, 15, 47, 60; *47*
    for weddings 69, 73; *68, 73*
    in baskets 30, 60; *61*
    wiring 73, 103; *73*
Presentation, flowers for 64, 65, 69; *65*
    see also Gifts
Preserving flowers and foliage 86, 88, 91, 92, 94, 96; *93-95*
Primroses 60; *60, 61*
Primulas 32, 44, 60, 65; *45*
Privet 18, 54, 65
Prolonging life of flowers and foliage 13-15, 104
    see also Preserving flowers
Protea 13
Protecting surfaces 15, 78, 104
Prunus 15
Pussy willow 35; *21*
Pyrethrums *17*

Quaking grass 86
Quince 15

Ranunculus 39, 67
Reception hall decorations 50
Reindeer moss 13
Retarding blossom 15
Rheum see Rhubarb
Rhododendrons 42, 67
Rhubarb 120; *120*
Ribbon
    and bouquets 65, 69, 73; *68*
    and posies 47, 60
    and swags 55, 58; *55*
Ribes see Flowering currant
Rock roses 67
Rosa mundi 67
Rosebay 67
Rosehips 16, 28, 56, 83; *19*
    preserving 94; *95*
Rosemary 42, 47, 54, 67, 69
Roses 12, 13, 15, 67, 120; *120*
    and bouquets 47, 64, 65, 73; *65, 72*
    and headdresses 70; *71*
    conditioning 12, 13, 14, 23
    in arrangements 37, 51, 79; *22, 29, 36, 50*
    preserving buds 86, 87, 92; *93*
    wiring 73; *73*
Rudbeckia 28, 67
Rue 67

Salads and flowers 44
Salvia 65, 67
Scabious 120-121; *120*
Scented lavender rings 64
Schefflera 81; *80*
Scissors 103, 105
Sea lavender *see* Statice
Sealing stems 14, 15, 96; *14*
Secateurs 103, 105
Seedheads 91, 108; *90*
    drying 86; *87*
Selecting material for arrangements 12, 13, 108, 109
Senecio 69
Settings and flowers 28, 32, 35; *31, 33, 34*
Sheaves of dried flowers 91; *90, 91*
Shells 32
    as containers 47, 102; *101*
Shepherd's parsley 52; *52*
Silica gel crystals 92, 103
Silver berry 113; *113*
Skeletonizing leaves 94; *94*
Snapdragons 67, 111; *111*
Snowdrops 30, 67; *21, 31*
Solomon's seal 14, 32
Special occasions and flowers 42, 47, 48, 78, 79; *79*
    see also Christmas, Easter, Weddings
Sprays of flowers
    as gifts 64
    bridal 69; *68*
    for presentation 65, 69; *65*
Spring flowers 60; *20, 21, 61*
Spruce 56; *57*
Statice 58; *58, 87*
    drying 86, 87
Stems
    cutting 12, 103, 110-121
    false 88, 103
    of dried flowers 88, 92
    treatments 12, 13, 14
    wiring 73, 103; *73*
Stocks 51, 67; *50*
Storage
    of dried flowers 88, 92
    of equipment 103
Straw daisies 110; *110*
Stub wires 103, 105
Sugar and roses 14
Summer flowers 23; *17, 22, 23*
    drying 86, 92; *87*
    see also Harvest festivals

Sun-bleaching process 96
Swags 42, 103
    Christmas 42, 58; *59*
    wedding 52, 54, 55; *55*
Sweet peas 67, 117; *19, 117*
Sweet William 67; *19*
Symmetrical arrangements 28, 102
Sympathy, flowers to express 66, 74, 75
Syringa 67, 121; *121*

Table decorations 39, 42
    and food 42, 44, 48; *45*
    Christmas 58; *58*
    for parties 42, 43, 48; *49*
    for weddings 42, 54, 55; *55*
Teazels 83
Thyme 67
Transporting flowers 14, 15, 64
Traveller's joy *see* Clematis
Tree peonies 32

Triangular arrangements 18, 64, 102; *19*
Trugs 30, 64, 100; *30*
Tulips 14, 67, 121; *21, 121*
    in arrangements 42, 56, 79, 81; *79, 80*
Twigs 28, 35, 56; *56, 57*

Valentine's Day flowers 47, 66; *47*
Vases 78, 100, 102
Verbascum 65
Verbena 44, 67
Vertical arrangements 102
    see also Pedestal arrangements
Viburnum 121; *121*
Vinegar and wild flowers 14
Violets 60, 67; *61*

Wall decorations 39, 74, 91; *39, 90, 91*

Wallflowers 67
Water
    and aftercare 14, 15, 104
    and hygiene 14
    see also Atomizers
Water-drying process 94; *94*
Weddings
    and anniversaries 42
    and decorations 42, 51, 52, 54, 55; *50, 53*
    bouquets and posies 69, 73; *68, 72, 73*
    headdresses 70; *70, 71*
    see also Church decorations
Wheat 28, 74, 83; *74, 83*
Whitebeam 15
Wild flowers 15, 23, 28, 54; *23*
    meanings of 66, 67
    prolonging life 14
Wild garlic 86; *87*
Willow 15
Wilting flowers 13

Window decorations 56, 78, 81; *57, 80, 81*
Winter flowers and goliage 15, 24, 56; *56, 57*
Wire 103, 105
Wire netting 104
    and hygiene 14
Wiring
    bouquets and posies 64, 73, 103; *73*
    concealing 103
    stems 73, 88, 103; *73, 88*
Wooden boards 35, 100, 103

Xeranthemums 67

Yucca 32

Zantedeschia aethiopica
    see Arum lilies
Zinnias 28, 42, 64, 67, 83
    preserving 94

ACKNOWLEDGMENTS

Photographic credits
Front cover by Pete Jones/ Holborn Studios

Back cover by Paul Williams

Nelson Hargreaves: 17, 19tl, 19cl, 19bl, 19br, 23, 29, 88, 101, 109

Nelson Hargreaves/Popular Gardening: 19tr, 36, 38, 52b, 74

Pete Jones/Holborn Studios: front cover, 6, 8-9

Paul Williams: back cover, 10t, 10bl, 10br, 11, 20, 21, 22, 24, 25, 26-27, 31, 33, 34, 39, 40-41, 43, 44-45, 46, 47, 49, 50, 52t, 53, 55, 56, 57, 58, 59, 61, 62-63, 65, 68, 71, 72, 75, 76-77, 79, 80, 82, 84-85, 87, 89, 90, 93, 95, 97, 98-99, 106-107

Photographs of plant portraits by: A–Z Collection, Heather Angel, K.A. & G. Beckett, Pat Brindley, Valerie Finnis, Brian Furner, Iris Hardwick Library, G.E. Hyde, IGDA, Harry

Smith Horticultural Photographic Collection, Michael Warren, Weed Research Organisation

The publishers would also like to thank the following people and companies for their contribution to this book:

for supplying merchandise for room sets: Designers Guild, Osborne & Little Ltd., and Marks & Spencer plc.

for baking the traditional sheaf-of-wheat harvest loaf — complete with mouse — on page 82: Albert Weaver, Master Baker, of Wethersfield, Braintree, Essex.

The glossary on page 66 has been culled from a variety of literary sources and in particular from *The Language of Flowers: an alphabet of floral emblems*, written by A Lady and published in 1857 by Thomas Nelson.